the discovery of happiness

the discovery of happiness

HAPPI-NESS

edited by stuart mccready

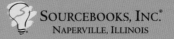
SOURCEBOOKS, INC.®
NAPERVILLE, ILLINOIS

contents

author biographies

Daud Ali

Writing on Nirvana and the Social Order (chapter two), Daud Ali is at the School of Oriental and African Studies, London. He studies courtly manners, romantic love and monastic discipline in early medieval India. His current work focuses especially on the history of social ethics in medieval Sanskrit literature.

Professor Wang Keping

Writing on Dao, Confucianism, and Buddhism (chapter three), Professor Keping is at the 2nd Foreign Language University, Beijing, and was visiting scholar at l'Université de Lausanne (1992-3), and the University of Toronto (1998-9). He is the holder of the British Academy K.C. Wong Fellowship and academic visitor at the University of Oxford (2000). Some of his major publications include: *Essays on the Sino-occidental Aesthetic Cultures* (1999); *The Classic of the Dao: A New Investigation* (1998); *Applied Aesthetics in Tourism* (1996), and *Sightseeing as an Aesthetic Activity* (1992).

Sara Sviri

Writing on both The Soul and the Intellect (chapter five) and Living in the Moment (chapter seven) is Sara Sviri. She is at the Department of Hebrew and Judaic Studies in University College, London. Her books are *Traveling the Path of Love: Sayings of Sufi Masters* and *The Taste of Hidden Things*.

Professor Naftali Loewenthal

Professor Loewenthal contributes a chapter on The Kabbalah and Hasidism (chapter six). He is at the Department of Hebrew and Jewish Studies, University College, London, where he lectures on Jewish Spirituality. He has written *Communicating the Infinite: The Emergence of the Habad School* (University of Chicago Press, 1990), and numerous articles on the history of Hasidism. He is married to Professor Kate-Miriam Loewenthal, who teaches Psychology at Royal Holloway London University. They are both Lubavitch Hasidim and have eleven children.

Lesley Smith

Writing on Heavenly Bliss and Earthly Delight (chapter eight), Lesley Smith is Academic Bursar, Dean, and Tutor in Politics at Harris Manchester College, Oxford. She has edited *Intellectual Life in the Middle Ages: Essays Presented to Margaret Gibson; Medieval Exegesis in Translation: Commentaries on the Book of Ruth*, and *Nicholas of Lyra: The Senses of Scripture.*

Jill Kraye

In chapter nine, Jill Kraye writes In Praise of Reason. She is Reader in the History of Renaissance Philosophy at the Warburg Institute, the School of Advanced Study, University of London. In addition, Jill Kraye is the associate editor of *The Cambridge History of Renaissance Philosophy* (Cambridge University Press, 1988); the joint-editor of *Pseudo-Aristotle in the Middle Ages* (Warburg Institute, 1986), *The Uses of Greek and Latin* (Warburg Institute, 1988), and *Humanism and Early Modern Philosophy* (Routledge, 2000); and the editor of *The Cambridge Companion to Renaissance Humanism* (Cambridge University Press, 1996), and *Cambridge Translations of Renaissance Philosophical Texts* (Cambridge University Press, 1997). In addition, she has published articles on the classical tradition in Renaissance philosophy.

Geoffrey Scarre

Writing on The Greatest Happiness of the Greatest Number in chapter ten, Geoffrey Scarre is Lecturer in Philosophy at the University of Durham. His books include *Utilitarianism* and *Logic and Reality in the Philosophy of J.S. Mill.*

Michael Argyle

Writing on Personality and Happiness (chapter eleven) is Michael Argyle, at Wolfson College Oxford, and Oxford Brookes University. He is Emeritus Reader in Experimental Psychology, University of Oxford, Emeritus Professor of Psychology, Oxford Brookes University, and Honorary Fellow, British Psychological Society. His books include *The Anatomy of Relationships; The Psychology of Interpersonal Behavior; The Social Psychology of Work; The Social Psychology of Leisure*, and *The Psychology of Religious Behavior, Belief and Experience.*

David Nias

David Nias is Senior Lecturer in Clinical Psychology at the Department of Human Science and Medical Ethics, St Bartholomew's and the Royal London School of Medicine, where he teaches clinical psychology to medical students. He contributes two chapters, on Managing Good and Bad Fortune (chapter twelve) and Strategies for Happiness (chapter thirteen). He has conducted research in abnormal, social, and sports psychology. He is coauthor of three books: *Love and Attraction* (with Glenn Wilson); *Sex, Violence, and the Media* (with Hans J. Eysenck); and *Astrology: Science or Superstition?* (also with Hans J. Eysenck). He now specializes in forensic psychology and gives evidence for court cases, parole boards, and mental health review tribunals.

Sir Anthony Kenny

Sir Anthony completes the book with Beyond A Warm Feeling (chapter fourteen). He is a Fellow of St John's College, Oxford, and Pro-Vice-Chancellor of the University of Oxford. He has been Warden of Rhodes House (1993-98); Master of Balliol College (1978-89), and President of the British Academy (1989-93). His books include: *The Oxford Illustrated History of Western Philosophy*; *Aristotle on the Perfect Life*; *A Brief History of Western Philosophy*; *Descartes: A Study of His Philosophy*; and *Action, Emotion, and Will.*

Stuart McCready

The editor of this series is Stuart McCready. He also writes the introductory chapter, In Pursuit of Happiness and chapter four, Pleasure, Happiness, and the Good. Stuart McCready has taken an interest in history across its entire span, from ancient Egypt to the twentieth century. Trained as a philosopher, he has taught in universities in Canada and Nigeria. He has also taught French and German in state and public boarding schools in England. During a thirty-year career in publishing, he has been executive editor on books covering a wide range of topics, including psychology, human behavior, natural history, health and medicine, warfare, theatre, astronomy, and art.

1: in pursuit of happiness Stuart McCready

An invitation to discovery

Smiling angel from Annunciation on the west portal of Reims cathedral, France.

Whatever was the beginning of this world, the end will be glorious and paradisiacal, beyond what our imaginations can now conceive Joseph Priestley

To explain why they think someone's happy, West Africans will often say, "You can see it on his body." In every other part of the world, as well, people can *see* happiness in others—when they have happy smiles on their lips, a distinctive crinkling around the eyes, and an open, cheerful way of standing or sitting. We can hear happiness in a cheerful tone of voice. A happy expression is universal: when psychologists showed pictures of American students, posing with various emotions, to isolated New Guinea Highlanders, they easily identified happy (as well as angry, sad, and disgusted) faces. It is nature that has genetically engineered us to communicate these basic feelings—without any example to follow, children born blind, deaf, and brain damaged smile, laugh, and cry.

Happiness and true happiness

Happiness is part of human nature—people from every background, even from the opposite ends of the Earth, are equally well acquainted with how it feels and are able to recognize it in each other. We readily understand a happy feeling as a good feeling to have, an unhappy feeling as a bad one. We are naturally inclined to prefer a happy life to a life of sorrow. It seems odd even to suggest that there is anything to discover about happiness.

Yet humanity returns again and again to the idea that instinct is not enough—that we also need wisdom about happiness. From 3,000 years of inquiry, this book assembles a rich selection of religious and philosophical insights and scientific findings. A recurring theme is the idea that the picture of happiness in the opening paragraph above is false, or that at most the happiness it captures is of little importance.

Daud Ali, for example, explains ancient philosophies and religions of India in which "true happiness" depends on liberation from the very needs and desires whose fulfillment normally gives us our familiar happy feeling. Wang Keping reveals how this idea, later adopted by the Chinese in the form of Buddhism, was prefigured in China by certain strands of Daoism that rejected a "false happiness"—an "enslavement to things"—in favor of "perfect happiness."

Chapter four explains why the most influential Greek philosophers, Plato and Aristotle, regarded everyday pleasures as being of little worth compared to philosophical contemplation. The Greek Stoics, for their part, taught that the only true happiness was to be found in reconciling ourselves to God's will. Sara Sviri and Jill Kraye show how these Greek ideas, combined with the belief that the ultimate bliss is knowing God, dominated the Western and Mediterranean worlds throughout the Middle Ages and the Renaissance.

Happiness in love—
Malari Ragini:
Lovers walk in the
country, Murshidabad
c.1770–75.

Coexisting with religious views that see true happiness as rather remote, there are very often mystical practices that aim at bringing this happiness into everyday life—though in its mystical conception it may differ deeply from the experience of nonpractitioners. Tali Loewenthal reveals the religious joy that is day to day living for Habad-Lubavitch Hasidic Jews. Sara Sviri explores Sufism, the mysticism of Islam. Lesley Smith gives us insights into medieval Christian mysticism.

Wisdom about worldly happiness

Throughout history, however, other thinkers have been glad to endorse the happiness pictured in the opening paragraph. Daud Ali touches on lost teachings of materialist philosophers in ancient India who upheld the pursuit of pleasure. Many of Wang Keping's Daoist and Confucian sages teach us about managing good and bad fortune and desire in a way that minimizes sorrow and enhances contentment.

The wisdom that these philosophers have to offer often amounts to advice about how to avoid the pitfalls that rob unwise people of the everyday happiness they seek. A text attributed to Democritus, the Greek materialist, for example, says that pleasure is what is good, but it warns us against harmful pleasures. The Greek word for pleasure is *hedone*, and so the term for this view is "hedonism." The point is to pursue pleasure without suffering the painful consequences of thoughtlessly enslaving yourself to pernicious pleasures (it is "rational hedonism"). The text also praises *euthumia* (cheerfulness, being of good spirit).

The Epicureans (who inherited Democritus's view that the world is a chance coming together of atoms) found no other meaning in life than pleasure and the avoidance of pain. A life of pleasure without pain, they taught, is the good we are talking about when we ask what a person's good is. The Epicureans lived a fairly austere life, shunning the pleasures of the world outside their communities, because they thought that self-indulgent pleasure leads to pain in the long run.

Hedonist philosophers are not the only ancients consulted for practical advice. It is possible to find wisdom in the Stoics's acceptance of what cannot be altered, or Plato's conviction that controlling appetites is a way of liberating ourselves, or Aristotle's ideas about fulfilling activity.

Happiness in the age of science

Geoffrey Scarre introduces another worldly philosophy. Utilitarianism is a doctrine that first captured the imagination of social reformers in the eighteenth century, the Age of Enlightenment. This doctrine holds that the criterion of an action's moral rightness or wrongness is whether it helps to maximize earthly happiness. Utilitarians believed that happiness (often equated with pleasure) is the good at which all action should aim. A reform of moral thinking was conceived along these lines. People were to use whatever wisdom was at hand when calculating how much happiness their actions were likely to produce. Science and technology were also envisaged as playing a crucial role in lifting the human race out of a sorry state into a much happier one.

Joseph Priestly (1733–1804) was an English chemist, Unitarian theologian, and sympathizer with the French Revolution. He emigrated to the United States, drawn in part by its express commitment to an inalienable human right to pursue happiness. Summing up the mood of expectation, he declared: "…whatever was the beginning of this world, the end will be glorious and paradisiacal, beyond what our imaginations can now conceive."

More than two centuries on, no one has yet developed a scientific way of calculating how much happiness an action or policy will produce, and people do not seem to feel very much happier. Social psychologists, however, have submitted happiness to a searching statistical analysis. Michael Argyle explains the methods and with David Nias reports on some of the key findings.

The Orrery, 1766. Joseph Wright's painting shows science being demonstrated to wondering members of the public.

What makes us happy?

Anyone hoping that properly instituted Utilitarian ethics and politics could have a paradisiacal outcome in terms of how we feel about our lives might easily be discouraged by the findings of psychology. Things that happen to us—especially anything so remote as the moral decisions of strangers or the policies of governments—seem to have little lasting effect on how we feel. More strongly correlated with happiness than anything else is personality, how easy you find it to enjoy other people's company, or how easily bothered you are by life's irritations. We are affected by good or bad luck, but after getting used to a change of luck, we all seem to have our own natural level of happiness to which we return, more or less. The factors in our environment that make the biggest lasting difference are ones that depend on *us*—we become happier by forming successful relationships, finding our work interesting, or doing something really satisfying as a leisure pursuit.

This research echoes a great many hunches that hedonists and other-worldly philosophers alike have had over thousands of years. Some Utilitarians would increase human happiness through better economic performances by nations, but almost all other philosophers and religious thinkers have surmised that the pursuit of wealth is not the true path to happiness. The research bears this out—in spite of rising standards of living, measurements of happiness since records began show no increase. Though the genuinely poor are less happy than average, there is not much difference between the amounts of happiness felt by people at widely divergent levels of income in the remaining social strata. Even lottery winners are no happier, within a year or so, than they were before their win.

Plato thought that a deep commitment to a significant other person is an unwise burden on the soul, but Confucius, Aristotle, and the Epicurians would feel confirmed by the statistical correlations that turned up in the twentieth century between happiness and personal relationships. Aristotle would make ready sense of the finding that being happy involves taking satisfaction from doing your job well. He would be particularly interested in the finding that the best opportunity to be happier is to be found in taking a critical look at how you use your leisure time, the time in which you are your own master.

Is happiness just pleasure?

We should not be too hasty in dismissing the achievements of the modern age. It is possible to miss improvements in happiness by adopting too narrow a concept. To begin with a relatively minor correction, there is much more to happiness than pleasure alone.

Pleasure-seeking on a public holiday: *The Fun of the Fair* by Charles Altamont Doyle (1832–93).

It's true that the picture of happiness with which this chapter opened is also a picture of pleasure. But, even if we think of happiness as a very ordinary—not especially philosophical or religious—condition, the picture is incomplete. You can be happy when you are not in any degree elated—even when you are asleep. All that is necessary is that you be satisfied with life, content with it, of a mind to say that life is good. There's not so much to picture in happy moments like this, but happy moments they are.

As Michael Argyle explains, psychologists often investigate happiness by asking people whether they feel sad, all right, happy, very happy, elated, and so on. Or they show them drawings of faces with varying degrees of happiness simply illustrated and ask them which expression best fits the way they feel. But this gives an indication only of what the psychologists call "emotional happiness." To get a more complete picture, they often ask people how *satisfied* they are with life.

Emotion always involves a general state of physical arousal. For this arousal to be felt as pleasure there has to be something more—our liking of, or welcoming of, the object of the arousal. Suppose a dim figure suddenly looms into view when you are alone, isolated, and vulnerable in an empty street at night. The raw material of your emotion is a heightened physical arousal as your body prepares you to act if necessary. Adrenaline goes into your bloodstream. Your heart beats faster. Your breathing quickens. You see the other person as a threat, and the emotion crystallizes as fear. But then you suddenly recognize the approaching figure as an old friend, and instantly the same arousal is felt as pleasure. The pleasure will be more or less intense (it will be delight, joy, or just feeling "pretty good") depending on how aroused you are. The emotion will be one of pleasure, rather than disgust, fear, or anger, depending on what the object of arousal means to you.

Happiness involves the liking, the welcoming, that is part of pleasure, but it is not focused on an object of arousal. It is rather a satisfaction with the overall situation. To feel pleasantly, delightfully, or joyfully aroused is normally also to feel happily aroused (we are satisfied with the circumstances in which we feel this way) and so, if someone asks, we typically say "I feel happy." And yet, even over these brief moments, happiness and pleasure are not the same thing. Pleasures can be experiences we enjoy but do not feel good about—we enjoy them guiltily— such as enjoying and, at the same time, regretting overeating. For an experience to be a pleasure, it is enough that we want it, and we can do this at the same time as wishing we didn't want it. But though we can imagine someone feeling pleasure while feeling genuinely guilty, it's harder to think of someone feeling happy while feeling genuinely guilty. This is part of what Plato had in mind when he thought of happiness as a harmony of the soul.

The happiness of the blessed

A more serious problem for our attempt to understand what happiness really is arises from the fact that words like "happy" and "happiness" are used in confusing ways.

In everyday life, the fact that we are talking about the happiness of a person almost invariably makes it plain that we mean a psychological feeling. Suppose you want to know if Margaret is happy. It matters whether Margaret would say so herself—her verbal expression of happiness ("I'm happy") ranks with the rest of her behavior (for example, how much she smiles) as prime evidence of her happiness. If she doesn't tamper with the evidence (she's not a skillful actress merely putting on a convincing but false display of happiness), we know what we need to know. She smiles and says "I'm happy," and no matter how bad things are for her objectively we haven't got a case for saying she's not happy. She might just have lost her job, but she is still happy—still satisfied with life— perhaps through blissful ignorance (no one has told her yet), or from just not caring ("I really didn't like that job anyway").

A girl leap frogs over her friend on a busy park's lawn.

When we speak of a happy turn of events, or a happy outcome, though, we normally mean by this something fortunate. What happened was for the better. If Margaret says that losing her job was a happy turn of events, it is possible to disagree with her by arguing about what is for the best.

Occasionally, even when we speak of happy people, we mean fortunate or blessed people, rather than people who have a certain subjective feeling. As Sir Anthony Kenny points out in chapter fourteen, that is how the Jerusalem Bible translates the Sermon on the Mount:

> *How happy are the poor in spirit;*
> *Theirs is the kingdom of heaven...*

Poetry also provides examples, such as this from Henry Wooten's *The Character of a Happy Life:*

> *How happy is he born and taught*
> *That serveth not another's will...*

We often also find this sense of "happy" in philosophy. In chapter three, for example, Wang Keping explains that happiness in the sense of the Chinese word *fu* is "good fortune" or (originally) "being in harmony with the gods." In the sense conveyed by *fu*, you can be happy without feeling it (for example, if you have just had a piece of good luck but no one has told you yet). Similarly, the Greek word *eudaimonia* is often translated by "happiness," but may also be translated by "the best life." It is very close to *fu*, meaning "favored by the gods," but is even more closely associated than the Chinese word with judging a whole life. Solon, the great Athenian law-giver of the sixth century B.C., is supposed to have said that you cannot call anyone happy until they are dead, because only then can their life be summed up and evaluated.

Making room for true happiness

Translators are not sloppy when they put "happiness" for *eudaimonia*. They are responding to the fact that the Greeks had no other word for happiness, and that "happiness" in our language is a highly flexible word. Even in the psychological sense of our word, you can drive out subjectivity simply by putting the word "true" in front. Margaret's being happy has to do with Margaret's feeling satisfied with life. "Margaret is happy" is as true as it can be if Margaret finds her life satisfactory. But "Margaret is truly happy," though it might sometimes mean no more than "Margaret is very happy," can mean that Margaret has discovered a happiness that is a model of what people seeking happiness should aim at.

Being truly happy would mean living a life that *is* good enough, rather than a life that merely *feels* good enough. It is not surprising, therefore, that so many philosophers have been concerned about true happiness—the person who merely feels happy might be of such an undemanding disposition as to be satisfied with almost any life at all, or so foolish as to be content with a life of crass pleasures when a more deeply satisfying life is within reach. As we shall see in chapter ten, even the leading nineteenth-century English utilitarian, John Stuart Mill, who thought that happiness is pleasure, was not prepared to accept that the good is whatever makes people *feel* satisfied. This would reduce utilitarianism to what he considered the absurdity of valuing *quantity* of pleasure over *quality* of pleasure. Pushpin—a popular children's game of the period—would be better than the poet Pushkin, because pleasure is available for so much less effort in playing the former than in reading the latter. Rather undemocratically, Mill proposed that pleasures be ranked for their value only by discerning people who were in a position to compare both common pleasures and more refined ones.

The happiness that is the good

The rarer sense of the word "happy," the one in which the happy are blessed, is still concerned with what is satisfactory. This sense goes further than "true happiness" in making feelings irrelevant. We could say something like "Happy is the life of the one called Margaret," meaning that her circumstances are particularly satisfactory, whether or not she thinks they are. However, no philosopher imagines that, in this sense of happiness, a happy person would fail to feel good about their life. Knowing happiness in the psychological sense is part of the happy condition of living a life that is happy in the sense of being fortunate. It is not necessary to have a positive psychological feeling about *everything* that is fortunate in life, however, so there will be aspects of the blessed life that are not included in its felt happiness.

In chapter fourteen, Sir Anthony Kenny offers a piece of twenty-first-century philosophy written especially for this book. In it he abandons the term "happiness" altogether—because of its psychological associations—and gives an account of what he takes to be our "well-being," by which he means our good. To be in Kenny's state of well-being is not just to feel happy, it is also to be in a happy circumstance. It includes not only happiness in the narrowly psychological sense but also objective circumstances that provide material welfare and bestow dignity. Ironically, Kenny's good is an easier one to improve on over the centuries than that of the hedonist. In spite of the fact that people adapt to progress and feel no happier, objective progress advances objective well-being.

You may, like Sir Anthony Kenny, prefer to avoid the confusion that arises from identifying happiness with a good that is not psychological. Even then, happiness and the good are likely to remain intimately entwined. The different elements into which Kenny divides well-being, for example, all relate to satisfaction. Even if you take health and material advantages for granted, the common experience of people who lose them is to feel unhappy about it, at least for a time. It is even harder to feel satisfied without objective support for one's self-esteem.

Michael Argyle points out that two of the main traits that make up a happy personality are a sense of personal control and a sense of self-esteem. He goes beyond statistics for a moment to say, "The relation is so close in fact that it may be better to regard self-esteem as part of satisfaction—satisfaction with the self." And this is surely so, for it would be a contradiction in terms to say that a person who was low in self-esteem felt happy, unless you were speaking of some brief moment of happiness when present pleasures have temporarily driven away a persistent sense of dissatisfaction.

People with strong personalities, who believe in themselves (in their own worth and their own effectiveness), have clung to a belief in themselves even in concentration camps during World War Two. Normally, however, there is some connection between how much control someone feels they have over their life and how much they have actually been given or have achieved. Similarly, self-esteem develops through your being treated with respect, or at least through having some rationale for thinking that the choices you make, and your personal values, make sense. Dignity—the most important element in Kenny's concept of well-being—fills in what a person so often needs in order to have self-esteem. It amounts to actual control, actual respect, and actually deserving respect.

When is it rational to feel happy?

Deserving respect is the component of dignity that Kenny introduces under the heading "value." It is his view that a condition for deserving respect, and so achieving an essential part of your own good is that "the life you lead must be a worthwhile one." (This means that Kenny is demanding at least as much of us as John Stuart Mill would—that we not fritter away our potentially valuable lives in trivial activity and then claim to have lived well.) It is thus a risky business to ask ourselves whether we've achieved our good. It involves reflecting on the possibility that we don't deserve to be as happy as we feel. And the possibilities for self-criticism, once we get started, are in fact much more profound than considering whether we are using our leisure in a worthwhile way.

Plato, who was right to say that happiness is a soul in harmony with itself, also said that such a soul could never embrace a shoddy or ugly system of values. Even the experience of the psychopath seems to bear this out. His self-esteem is based on the conviction that other people (if they were not shackled by convention) would admire his cleverness in getting away with outrages and admire the power he exerts over victims. It does not serve his self-esteem to doubt that cleverness and the power to inflict pain are admirable qualities, and he uncritically makes do with any argument to dismiss this doubt.

Most of us have much more mildly defective selves to protect, but a certain amount of irrationality (in the form of uncritical self-appraisal) serves us all. In chapter eleven, Michael Argyle mentions the statistically proven fact that people are happier when they don't fret about whether they *should* be happy. Sir Anthony Kenny, too, gives a warning. At the end of chapter fourteen, he points out that by learning to be more discerning about what is worthwhile, it is possible to take to heart standards that we find increasingly difficult to fulfill.

An influential twentieth century theory of value might come to our rescue here—one implying that if you are happy with your life, there is no way of sensibly raising the question of whether you *should* be happy with it. This is the teaching that judgments of value are emotive—they are ultimately a matter of expressing happiness or discontent with the object evaluated. (Some philosophers say they are also prescriptive—in making one, you show that you feel like committing yourself to choosing the valued object in practice, and also that you wish other people would choose such objects.) Armed with this view, when someone says you are not experiencing true happiness because you have left out the joy of knowing God, or the self-respect nonpsychopaths get from treating other people decently, or the pleasure of reading poetry from nineteenth-century Russia, there is no reason why you should pay them any attention.

Yet argued criticism of a way of life has had proven success in changing people's minds about how they should live and in making them happier. This is how some of the therapies David Nias outlines in chapter thirteen work. Unhappy people are persuaded that it makes sense to think more positively about themselves, other people, and the circumstances in which they live. They are channeled into objectively improving their circumstances by making more social contacts and setting achievable goals for themselves in activities they enjoy. This gives them a greater sense of control over their lives and better self-esteem. They are directed to what has worked well for other people and to learning to enjoy the benefits other people have learned to appreciate.

Reflection about what it makes sense to value and about what has made other people happy can help unhappy people, and so long as it is not done in a gloomy way, there is no reason why it should not further enrich the lives of happy people. We do not even need to submit to the authority of discerning experts to learn that we can use our leisure better. Psychologists who ask ordinary people like us what our lives are like and whether we are happy, have built a statistically proven case for saying that passively watching television is less rewarding than putting something of yourself into a goal-directed activity that involves active participation with other people.

Philosophers and religious teachers who invite us to look even more deeply into our souls for the happiness that deserves the name invite us on a more difficult journey—along a road to what ought to be valued. Even after all these millennia, it remains poorly charted. We do not even know where the knowledge is to come from that one or another way of life actually deserves more respect, nor whether it makes sense to ask such a question. If it is right to extend this invitation, then for each of us there is a rather intriguing missing piece in the complex picture of happiness this book presents. That is the happiness—the true happiness—that we have not yet discovered.

2: nirvana and the social order Daud Ali

Happiness in Indian philosophy and religion

A smiling Nepalese rendering of Gautama the Buddha.

Monks, all sensation, whether pleasant or painful is burning with the fire of lust, hate, and delusion. It is burning with birth, age and death, with sorrows, lamentations, pains, griefs, and despairs Buddha

In the long history of India, the best-articulated views about what should be considered happiness came from a surprisingly small number. These were a group of men whose lifestyles differed quite considerably from that of the great majority of people.

The Veda tradition

The earliest sources in India—the orally preserved hymns, formulas, and incantations (c.1500–500 B.C.) which later came to be known as the Veda, were the work of a conspicuously separate class of professional priests. The great orthodox philosophical traditions which later evolved in Indian history, all grounded their knowledge in the authority of the Veda and the society it sanctioned.

The society, as far as it can be reconstructed from the orthodox texts, was founded on a hierarchical division of roles which placed the priestly, royal, and property-owning estates above the great mass of people who were deemed unfit for knowledge and refinement. The result was that the humanistic basis of Indian philosophy, which made possible the theorization of the goals and ends of human life, was actually built firmly upon a divided society.

First reflections on happiness

Strictly speaking, the first rigorous conceptions of happiness in India followed the transformation of the Veda. The incantations, formulas, and hymns of the Veda were all composed with the end of performing the sacrifice—which was to bring fame, cattle, and sons to the sacrificer. Occasionally, happiness is mentioned in the hymns sung to the gods, but we find no theory of what happiness is. By contrast, the last texts of the Vedas, known as the *Upanisads*, are philosophical reflections in which new ideas evolved. They were composed in the context of growing urbanization and newly emerging social roles. Wealthy urbanites were complemented by those who eschewed property ownership in the pursuit of moral and spiritual perfection. These men organized themselves into orders or wandered individually and depended on men of society for their livelihood. They laid the groundwork of early Indian philosophical reflection, and may be considered the first great theorists of happiness in India.

Though they represent the seeds of later speculative philosophy in India, the *Upanisads* marked the first rumblings of a far greater revolution. They were the first explicit speculations on the existence, nature, and capacities of the human self in early India. But they were overshadowed by the meteoric rise of Buddhism in northeastern India, from the fifth century B.C. on. Buddhism consciously posed itself against the Vedic

An eighteenth-century Indochinese hanging scroll showing the Buddha inaugurating the practice of receiving alms.

sacrifice, and was able to give a much more systematic expression to the growing speculation in society. And so Indian philosophy, though it may have returned to the *Upanisads* for its doctrines, really became a systematic body of thought through the influence of Buddhism.

Nirvana and Buddhism

The Buddhists began their discussion of the human condition, not with how a man should attain happiness, but rather, how he should avoid unhappiness or suffering. Attaining happiness, in other words, was the end result of escaping the more fundamental and general condition of suffering. For Buddhists and later Indian philosophers alike, each human self lived through a wearisome plethora of births which varied according to the fruit of his actions. These births, with their highs and lows, constituted a vast trap or net which afflicted the self. The highest goal of ethical and spiritual striving was therefore to pass beyond the vicissitudes of suffering by identifying its causes and means of eradication. The four noble truths of Buddhism put the problem well: all life is suffering, and the root of suffering is thirst, the eradication of thirst thus leads to the eradication of suffering. The cessation of suffering was called "liberation"—*nirvana* or *moksa*—by Indian philosophers.

Worldliness and enjoyment

Buddhist theories of human liberation contained within them an implicit criticism of what may be called "limited" happiness. Sensual enjoyments, feelings of delight and pleasure which were experienced by the self in the world of rebirths, were most often designated by the Sanskrit term *sukha* (happiness). Related terms covered gladness, joy, and satisfaction. All these, though temporarily gratifying, were deemed to lead to increased suffering. The Buddhists' disciplinary codes constantly declare that monks were to avoid the ways of the "householders, who enjoy the pleasures of the senses." Such happinesses led the individual to become ever more "attached" to fleeting or "conditioned" realities which would inevitably disappear. Chief among these attachments, for Buddhism, was the very idea of a permanent and unchanging self. Abandoning the thirst for a permanent and stable soul was the highest and most fundamental goal of early Buddhist practice. On the other hand, for the later Hindu philosophies, which based themselves on the *Upanisads*, the most important goal was to recognize the utter independence of the soul from its external surroundings and to recognize its nondifference from the universal principle. In either case, the experience of worldly happiness was denigrated as transient and fleeting.

An illustration from the Rajasthan manuscript *The Rose Garden of Love.*

Into the *manas*

Psychologically, the experience of pleasure and happiness occurred in a part of the self called the *manas*, a term whose meaning defies precise translation in English, but which may be approximated by the words "heart" and "mind." The mind was considered to be one of the "outer" and inessential or impermanent parts of the self for most Indian philosophers—more akin to the body than the soul. It was considered to be an "internal organ"—a place where feelings of both happiness and suffering, rooted in the self's contact with the external world, were experienced. The soul's experience of happiness and suffering was termed "enjoyment." This enjoyment was the very opposite of release. Enjoyment meant the experience of the world of rebirths, which offered only limited happiness.

The art of romantic liaisons: Krishna and Radha, from the *Gita Govinda* series from around 1780.

Those who follow the world

Though the early philosophers of India, in their pursuit of the ultimate goal of human striving, criticized worldly happiness as ephemeral, this does not mean that ancient Indian culture rejected happiness in the world altogether. Physical pleasure and material wealth were recognized as legitimate goals of human life, and their measured and disciplined pursuit was to bring happiness in the form of success and satisfaction—through the acquisition and enjoyment of money, the courtly arts of refined conversation and connoissieurship, games and sports, and, of course, romantic liaisons. Some philosophers, known as the *Lokayatas* (literally "those who follow the world"), denied the existence of the soul or of any liberative states like *nirvana*. The only sure existents were those which could be demonstrated to the senses. Completely absent were the concepts of enjoying the fruit of one's actions in future lives and restraining oneself from overattachment to the world through one's senses. In a world where all that was beyond the senses was denied, the only legitimate goal was the pursuit of the sense-objects.

Who these philosophers were remains shrouded in mystery, as they are known to us only from the writings of their detractors. Sporadic evidence seems to suggest that experts in this "materialistic" philosophy were sometimes called upon for their practical knowledge by mainstream Hindus, particularly at royal courts. Though formally their numbers must have been small, and none of their own treatises have come down to us, their detractors consistently mention that *Lokayata* was the default philosophy current among the masses.

Heavenly felicity, moral perfection

Related to worldly happiness was heavenly enjoyment. The heavens were an important part of both Buddhist and Hindu cosmology. They were enjoyed by men and women who performed meritorious deeds during their lives and adhered to the ethical laws. For most philosophers, they formed part of the great cycle of worldly life, and as such were considered to be part of conditioned existence. They must therefore be sharply distinguished, in the case of Buddhism, from liberation. After enjoying the reward of heaven for a specified time, the individual self returned to human birth. Nevertheless, the felicities of heaven, usually termed *sukha*, are instructive, as they are ever subtler and lighter than those of the gross material world and reveal an important value structure.

In Buddhist texts, we find descriptions of heavens akin to palaces and gardens, but composed of finer objects. They were filled with wondrous trees whose flowers emitted beautiful fragrant smells and never faded. Other trees were composed of gems and granted all wishes. Sex and

The winds are greatly agitated and blowing everything in the four quarters, shake and drive many beautiful, graceful and many-colored stalks of gem trees, which are perfumed with sweet heavenly scents, so that many hundred beautiful flowers of delightful scent fall down on the earth, which is full of jewels Sukh'vativyèha

eating were not necessary, and their inhabitants traveled about in subtler physical forms. In the Buddhist heavens, the afflictions of lust, hunger, and thirst, which accompanied grosser pleasures, were absent. In one Buddhist text, the occupants of heaven are described as simply watching the eternal blooming of trees and plants. These heavens, while not the ultimate goal of spiritual practice, were considered the finest form of pure worldly enjoyment and can be seen as a projection of what was deemed felicitous in this culture.

Bliss and soul

Many Hindu philosophers ultimately distanced themselves from worldly happiness whether earthly or heavenly. They also recognized that *nirvana* could be conceived of as a final happiness—an ultimate bliss that was synonymous with moral or spiritual perfection. The philosophy expounded eloquently by Samkara in the eighth century A.D. asserted the identity of the human soul with the world principle (*brahman*), and considered bliss to be identical with the soul. As the *Taittiriya Upanisad* puts it, "*brahman* itself is bliss," for *brahman* was the profound delight of liberation. In such philosophies, worldly happiness was based on external objects, whereas final liberation was the realization of a bliss that was entirely intrinsic and pre-existent in the soul from the beginning. Ultimate bliss was not obtained as much as realized as an existing aspect of the soul, independent of any contact with the exterior world.

Krishna in cosmic form, from Rajasthan in 1890.

Theistic philosophies

In contrast to such idealist quietism were the great theistic movements which dominated India from the first centuries of the Christian era. They saw either the god Shiva or Visnu as an omnipotent and omniscient cosmic lord. Ultimate happiness was conceived of as a juxtaposition or partial absorption of the individual soul with that of the Godhead. Happiness here was not grounded in the being of the individual human soul alone but resided rather in the relationship between that soul and its lord and source.

While distinctions were made between mundane and spiritual bliss, theistic philsosophy borrowed heavily from the vocabulary of human relationships to describe ultimate bliss. The relation between the human soul and God was imagined as lover and beloved, parent and child, and slave and master. Ultimate release, or liberation, for the theistic philosophies, was typically imagined as the arrival of the individual soul at God's residence, where it devotedly contemplated its master. This less abstract notion of human happiness had important social implications. If theistic happiness borrowed heavily from the vocabulary of human relations, it in turn had the potential to infuse these relations with its own hierarchical trappings.

Happiness in this world was explicitly linked to the assumption of particular social roles. The idealization of servitude, for example, as a state of happiness, was reflected in the medieval social order. If in the theistic religions devoted service was elevated as both a means to ultimate bliss and bliss itself, it is no wonder that a medieval manual on the relations between servants and masters exhorts servants to be happy and content in their service. It would seem that the philosopher's final bliss in India was far more attached to the world than it would care to have admitted.

Shiva was the cosmic lord, here seen as part of the Holy Family of Shiva and Parvati on Mount Kailash.

The beings, if touched by those winds which blow perfume with various scents, are as full of happiness as a Bhikshu who has obtained nirvana Sukhʻvativyèha

3: dao, confucianism, and buddhism Wang Keping

Happiness in Chinese philosophy and religion

A cheerful ax-head: based on the design of a blade from northern China.

To him there is no distinction
Between low and high position
Between poverty and wealth
He is poor but has no sorrow
He has been a happy man Shao Yong

Outdoors during the Chinese Spring Festival (*chun jie*) the ear-splitting crack of fireworks fills the air. Indoors, the Chinese character *fu* (happiness in the sense of "good fortune") in brightly colored cut-paper or ink-brush calligraphy, glitters everywhere. In Chinese philosophy and religion, both *fu* and *le* (joy) are key concepts of happiness. Yet it is *le* rather than *fu* that is more frequently and widely pondered by all the three major schools of Chinese thought: Daoism (Taoism), Confucianism, and Buddhism.

Good fortune and misfortune

It is simply common sense for people to seek *fu* (happiness or good fortune), and to avoid *huo* (misfortune or calamity). But the majority of the Chinese are familiar with such old sayings as, "Extreme happiness may turn into sadness" (*le ji sheng bei*), and "Bitter experience may result in sweet joy" (*ku jin gan lai*). So when people are feeling on top of the world because of an extraordinary blessing, they are intuitively conscious of the downhill movement toward the opposite side, and try to keep their emotion within a temperate range. If they are plunged into a dreadful plight, they retain hope and make continuous efforts toward a positive outcome.

The Chinese seem to play with the polarity of *fu* and *huo* with their will as well as their intellect. They handle it with a kind of practical wisdom that is largely drawn from the teachings of the Daoist philosopher Lao Zi (Lao-tzu), who may have lived at about 500 B.C.: "Misfortune is that beside which fortune lies; Fortune is that beneath which misfortune lurks." The interplay between fortune and misfortune can be dramatic, as illustrated by the following anecdote:

> There lived an old man near China's northern borders. When his horse wandered into the territory of the tribes to the north, all his neighbors commiserated with him over the loss. "Perhaps this will turn out to be a blessing," said the old man. After a few months, the horse came back accompanied by a mare from the north. Seeing this, all his neighbors congratulated him. "Perhaps this will turn out to be a misfortune," claimed the old man. He prospered and had many fine horses. One day, his son, who was fond of riding, fell from a horse and broke his leg. All the neighbors came to commiserate with the family. "Perhaps this will turn out to be a blessing," thought the old man. One year later, the northern tribes mounted an invasion of the border regions. All able bodied young men were

Pictures of happiness

The character for the Chinese word *fu* (happiness, good fortune) has two parts—its left-hand side evolved from an ancient pictogram of a man sacrificing to the gods, and its right-hand side evolved from an ancient pictogram of a table piled high with wealth. Its form therefore straddles two spheres: the religious and the material, and so *fu* implies both spiritual and material well-being. The character for *huo* (misfortune) also shows a man sacrificing on the left, but on the right his prayers are answered by a symbol for calamity.

In addition to *fu* and many others, there is another important Chinese term for happiness—*le* (joy). The same character also represents the word *yue*. The primary meaning of *yue* is music, but *le* and *yue* feature in a significant interplay of effect according to the Confucian doctrine of music. *Le* is an inner feeling by which the creation of music is inspired, and *yue* evinces joy in the audience. Joy in this context is both a psychological state and an aesthetic response.

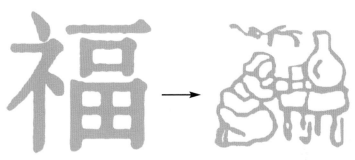

Fu (happiness, good fortune)

The *Fu* character is derived from this pictogram

Huo (ill fortune)

Le (happiness, joy)

enlisted to fight against the invaders except for the old man's son, because he was crippled. The father and his son thus survived the consequent slaughter.

The lesson of this story is that an apparent blessing can often be a misfortune in disguise, and vice versa. Fortune and misfortune are opposites in an interactive or transformational circle. One should see through the positive surface and keep alert to the potentially negative aspects of events and circumstances. One should not take any blind or harsh action, but try to stop one's action at the right place in order to keep things from reversing to the unfavorable side. This requires a high awareness of the principle that "The reversal is the moment of the *Dao*." One must always be conscious of how the positive and negative work together and change around, which is the "inevitable reversal of the extreme" (*wu ji bi fan*).

The Chinese believe that, as the principle of all principles, the *Dao* moves in a dynamic and circular fashion, and all things determined by the *Dao* are part of an everchanging process. One has no control over the transformation between opposites unless one succeeds in attaining the *Dao*. Only then are opposites such as fortune and misfortune reduced to their original state of unity.

Lao Zi believed "the reversal" is an automatic and absolute feature of reality. This might seem to nurture a passive attitude, as though initiative or endeavor would have no effect. But fortune can turn only into misfortune (and the other way around) under proper conditions. Otherwise, things will remain what they are.

Happiness as contentment

Happiness comes from the satisfaction of a desire while unhappiness comes from its frustration. Yet, human desires are difficult to satisfy in their totality for the satisfaction of a single desire will give rise to more desires. This is like cutting off one corner of a rectangular desk: each cut gives the desk more corners rather than fewer corners.

What can be done with this paradox of reducing desires by satisfying desires? There is a saying cherished among the Chinese: "One who is content (with what one has) is always happy" (*zhi zu zhe chang le*). Its implied message is that the fewer desires you have, the more easily you will be satisfied, and accordingly, the more happiness you are likely to realize. This thought can be traced back to Lao Zi's philosophy of contentment. First, he claims, "He who is content will encounter no disgrace" (*Zhi zu bu rou*). Second, he affirms that, "He who is content with knowing contentment is always content indeed" (*zhi zu zhi zu, chang zu yi*). The argument for the first claim is pointed to a comparative value judgment with respect to life, fame, and wealth. In human society, many people become so acquisitive that they recklessly pursue fame and wealth. They confine themselves to "the reins of fame and the shackles of wealth" (*ming jiang li suo*), unable to see that, "An excessive love of fame is bound to cause an extravagant expense (of vital energy); a rich hoard of wealth is bound to suffer a heavy loss (in case of robbery, burglary, or murder for property)."

He who is content with knowing contentment is always content indeed Lao Zi

Zhi zu zhi zu, chang zu yi

View of the Summer Palace, Beijing.

Lao Zi recommended the virtue of being content with what one has at hand. In this way, one can be free from disgrace, danger, or loss. This is an extension of the idea that runs: "He who is contented is rich" (*zhi zu zhe fu*). Those who are content are most apt to live a life filled with tranquillity, peace, and spiritual nourishment.

Contentment is contrasted with desires, discontent, and covetousness. Lao Zi held, "There is no guilt greater than lavish desires. There is no calamity greater than discontent. There is no defect greater than covetousness." Arbitrary as it may sound, the sharp critique and preaching tone reinforce the significance of contentment.

Being "content with knowing contentment" has two aspects: there is practically elementary contentment when one is content with what one has; then there arises a higher reflective contentment when one is content with knowing one's contentment. It is on the basis of initial contentment that the higher contentment is possible through a higher level of personal cultivation.

All in all, the message of contentment appeals to those who are frustrated or depressed with an over-competitive and greed-ridden style of life. Of course, Lao Zi's ideal does not prevent one from doing what one can do and becoming what one can become. His teaching was not meant to justify being passive or just plain lazy.

Meditating on perfection, a Daoist mystic (the fifteenth-century artist T'ang Yin), depicts his purified self floating in the air, while his earth-bound self dreams at the window of a thatched hut in the mountains.

The great and the small

Prominent among Chinese thinkers from antiquity onward is Zhuang Zi (*Chuang Tzu*), a Daoist philosopher whose thoughts were written down in the third century B.C. He was fond of using anecdotes to illustrate his ideas. In *The Happy Excursion* (*Xiao yao you*) he wrote:

> *In the Northern Ocean there is a fish called kun, which is many thousand miles in size. This fish metamorphoses into a bird called peng, whose back is many thousand miles in breadth. When the bird rouses itself and flies, its wings obscure the sky like clouds…When it is moving to the Southern Ocean, it flaps along the water for 3,000 miles… When it ascends to the height of 90,000 miles, the wind is all beneath it. Then, with the blue sky above, and no obstacle on the way, it mounts upon the wind and starts for the south… A cicada and a young dove laugh at the peng, saying: "When we make an effort, we fly up to the trees. Sometimes, not able to reach there, we fall to the ground midway. What is the use of going up 90,000 miles in order to fly toward the south?"… A quail also laughs at it, saying: "Where is that bird going? I spring up with a bound, and when I have reached no more than a few yards I come down again. I just fly about among the brushwood and the bushes. It is also perfect flying…" This is the difference between the great and the small.*

What the story suggests is ambiguous. On the one hand, we see the enormous difference between the great and the small in their features and pursuits. The *peng* has large wings and flies high and far. The cicada and quail have tiny wings, and low and short flight. Accordingly, the great and small experience and achieve different things. This is also true of what they each need and enjoy. If they all go against nature by imitating each other in their way of life, distress and frustration will certainly arise. In consequence, satisfaction is relative.

On the other hand, we find that the great and small are different by nature. They move and live in distinct ways because they simply follow their own nature and act in accord with their inborn capacity. They both indulge in what they are doing and enjoy themselves to their full extent. Such satisfaction can be equal if no distinction is made between superior and inferior. It is just like two guests who are equally pleased at a royal banquet even though one has a big appetite and the other has a small one. Zhuang Zi often advocated his notion of "equalizing all things" (*qi wu*) as the fundamental principle of his philosophy.

Perfect happiness

Zhuang Zi argued that, "Perfect happiness is without happiness" (*zhi le wu le*). This paradoxical way of putting things was possible because he distinguished perfect happiness (*zhi le*) from happiness (*le*).

To understand *zhi le*, one must come to terms with *le*. This happiness is derived totally from what the world values, such as riches, honors, longevity, benevolence, easy living, good food, splendid clothes, beautiful companions, and fascinating music. Those who seek these things believe that they can find happiness. They slavishly imitate the majority, as if this were their only choice. Zhuang Zi grew skeptical about the value of that happiness. He denied that it is true happiness, and treated it as a hollow vanity or a self-chosen burden. He went on to argue:

> *The rich who toil to accumulate more money than they can ever spend, do they not stray too far from the point of preserving their physical existence? The nobility who work day and night with anxiety and painstaking efforts to secure their positions, do they not fail to take care of their physical existence? And since human kind is inevitably born to grief, does it not mean prolonged grief if one should have the misery and suffering to live a long life?*

All this is due to his sharp observation of the human condition in his time, when many fell victim to material fetishism or social alienation, and they were blinded and "enslaved by things (external to the real value of life)" (*ren wei wu yi*). Like many in his time, they sacrificed their quality of life for a false notion of happiness.

Perfect happiness goes beyond common values and consequently comes into effect in the absence of false happiness. It is a state of mind purified of all desires and emancipated from any confinement. It is the complete accomplishment of the *Dao* of "taking no action" (*wu wei*), featuring absolute spiritual freedom and independent personality. This perfect happiness transcends any distinction between happiness and unhappiness, and even between life and death. It can be exemplified by another anecdote. When Zhuang Zi's wife died, he felt great sadness at first. Later he was found playing a melody on a bowl and singing joyfully when his friend came over to offer condolence. He was criticized for his contrary behavior. But he explained that his wife had returned to the original state of being; her *qi*, vital energy, had dispersed and was flowing freely between the sky and the earth, as if sleeping soundly in a cosmic chamber.

In Zhuang Zi's view, life and death are natural phenomena determined by the gathering and dispersing of *qi*. If one sees through the true nature of life and death and embraces happiness and unhappiness alike, one is closer to perfect happiness.

Three types of joy

If we turn from Daoism to Confucianism, we note that Confucius (551–479 B.C.) and his successor Mencius (372–289 B.C.) were preoccupied with a practical approach to happiness. They both charted out "three types of joy" in daily life.

According to Confucius, one who enjoys doing three kinds of things will stand to benefit. One should "take pleasure in the correct regulation of the rites and music, in singing the praises of others' goodness, and in having a large number of excellent fellows as friends." The first category is associated with promoting religious rites in order to develop social order and with educating oneself in music for the sake of personal cultivation. The second category leads to appreciating the good conduct of others and learning from it. The third category involves making friends of gentlemanly character or virtuous personality, because one is influenced and judged by the companions one keeps. In contrast, many people prefer three other kinds of things: "showing off, living a dissolute life, and indulging in food and drink." They are destined to encounter negative consequences in their lives because exhibitionism invites trouble, extravagance corrupts the spirit, and excessive love of sensuous pleasures harms one's health.

Over a century later, Mencius recommended that, "A gentleman delights in three things… His parents are alive and his brothers are well. This is the first delight. Above, he is not ashamed to face Heaven; below, he is not ashamed to face man. This is the second delight. He has the good fortune to have the most talented pupils in the Empire. This is the third delight." The first delight couples the feeling of family affection with piety and love. The second delight lies in fulfilling one's mission in both spiritual and social domains. The third delight reflects the joyful and sincere feelings of a successful teacher.

Both Confucian joy and Mencian delight conceal a moral code and a commitment to personal cultivation and social service. Regarding the three kinds of joy concerned in each case, there arises such a value scale: your love of practicing them is superior to your mere knowledge of them; and your pleasure in practicing them is superior to your mere love of practicing them. The pleasure experienced here is more than a natural outcome of what is gained from a good-natured action. It is usually inward, disinterested, and extremely practical.

The delighted pursuit of love

The search for happiness was one of the primary objectives of the Neo-Confucianism of the Song Dynasty (960–1279), which encouraged a self-conscious reflection on "the happiness of Confucius and Yan Hui" (*Kong–Yan le chu*).

This happiness was explored in two commonly quoted remarks by Confucius. One is about Confucius himself: "With coarse rice to eat, with only water to drink, and my elbow for a pillow, I find happiness in them. Wealth and honor attained through immoral means have as much to do with me as passing clouds." The other is about his favorite disciple Yan Hui: "How admirable Hui is! A bowlful of rice to eat, a gourdful of water to drink, and living in a mean dwelling; all this is a hardship others would find intolerable, but Hui does not allow this to affect his joy. How admirable Hui is!"

How would happiness be practiced in such harsh living conditions? First, Confucius and Yan Hui could be optimists, if not escapists, holding fast to an attitude to the reality that deliberately neglected their plight (*le tian pai*). Second, they could be highly self-contained, not simply content with what they were, but accepting whatever destiny brought to them (*le tian zhi ming*). Lastly, since they were so delighted in their pursuits of the *Dao*, they either forgot about their poverty-stricken conditions or freed themselves from cares and worries (*an ping le dao*). In fact, what they really set their hearts on was enlightenment from the *Dao*, for which they would even be ready to lay down their lives. As Confucius claimed, "If I am told about the *Dao* in the morning, I will be happy even when passing away in the evening."

What is the *Dao* that they pursued? It is the *Dao* of *ren*, the cardinal Confucian virtue. In his terms, *ren* is "loving people" (*ai ren*). Initially, *ren* starts with the family members, involving piety to the old and affection for the young. Then it is extended to neighbors and communities. It is achieved by following two maxims:

(1) Do not impose on others what you yourself do not desire.

(2) Help others establish themselves in so far as you wish to establish yourself; and help others achieve their goals in so far as you wish to achieve yours

The first maxim expects you to put yourself into the situation of others. What you ought to do to others is just what you wish for yourself. This will foster unselfishness by avoiding benefiting oneself alone at the expense of the interests and feelings of others. The second maxim advises you to broaden your mind and abide by the rules of fair play. For only by doing so can we reduce egoism and maximize our development. This kind of *ren* is equivalent to fraternity, but it can be further developed to the supreme level of "loving people and treasuring things" (*ren min ai wu*). At this point,

Confucius the philosopher (551–479 B.C.) from a 1922 illustration.

the *Dao* of *ren* is turned into universal love, not only toward human beings, but also encompassing all things in the universe.

It would be wrong to conclude that Confucius made no distinction between poverty and wealth, or never bothered about being poor or rich. Actually, he stressed that poverty and low status are what men dislike, while wealth and high status are what men desire. But if one cannot become rich and honored in the righteous way, one should remain carefree and enjoy one's life as it is. Confucius was always ready to improve his material condition and once admitted that he would be willing to work as a guard holding a whip outside the marketplace if it were possible for him to get wealth by doing so. Otherwise, he would follow his own preferences in learning and pursuing the *Dao*.

In short, "the happiness of Confucius and Yan Hui" is chiefly attributed to a conscientious devotion to the *Dao* of *ren* and also to a firm sense of self-dignity in the face of hardships. Such a spirit is peculiar to the "gentleman" (*jun zi*), a personality idealized throughout Confucianism and expressed by Mencius as the "great man" (*da zhang fu*), "who cannot be led into seeking excessive pleasures when wealthy and honored, or deflected from his pursuit of the *Dao* when poor and obscure, nor can he be made to bend himself humbly before superior powers." Following their doctrines, the Neo-Confucianist Shao Yong became enlightened and shaped his way of life as depicted in his *Song of Happiness*:

> ...(To him there is no distinction)
> Between low and high position,
> Between poverty and wealth...
> He is poor but has no sorrow,
> He drinks, but never to intoxication.
> He gathers the springtime of the world into his mind.
> He lives by a small pond and enjoys reading poetry...
> Yet he is one with Heaven and Earth.
> He cannot be conquered by a great army.
> He cannot be induced by a great salary.
> Thus he has been a happy man,
> For sixty-five years.

A laughing Buddha rests in a cave sculpted out of the wall of Feilai Feng, a rock formation on the grounds of the Lingyin Temple in Hangzhou, China. The rock formation is famous for its fine sculptures of Buddhist scenes.

The great man cannot be led into seeking excessive pleasures when wealthy and honored Mencius

Paradise and sudden enlightenment

After its introduction into China from India in the first century, Buddhism continued to develop and branched into eight major sects up until the Tang Dynasty (618–906). Of all the sects, the *Chan* (*Zen, dhyana*) Buddhism remains the most influential.

Buddhism as a whole perceives life as the fountainhead of suffering, and even likens it to "a bitter sea" (*ku hai*). In contrast, it offers a "world of supreme happiness" or "paradise of Buddhahood" (*ji le shi jie*). Its plan for achieving happiness is portrayed in *sutras* such as this:

> *In this world all the rivers refresh the spirit. Their water has many sweet fragrances. Bunches of flowers decorated with all imaginable jewels float along on it, and their rustling is full of sweet music. All the beings there are free from any misery but enjoy happiness of any conceivable kind. There are no signs of sin, misfortune, distress, sadness, and mortality. There is no sound of pain, and not even the sound of a feeling that is neither pain nor joy. Whatever they wish to eat is easily available and their bodies and spirits delight in it…*

There are further elaborations, all representing paradise as too joyful to be inhabitable, even by worshippers who crave it. For this pragmatic reason, *Chan* Buddhism has created a simpler alternative that is accessible to its practitioners. It is called "sudden enlightenment" (*dun wu*). This enlightenment is a special kind of wisdom, based on the negation of the phenomenal world and on the belief that everyone by nature has the possibility of Buddhahood or Buddhata—the potential *bodhi*, or innate ability to attain wisdom or *prajna*. Sudden enlightenment requires that one should not be distracted by anything external—this is the foundation that leads to freedom. It also requires an "absence of thought," meaning that one is not carried away by thinking in the process of thought.

According to the sixth Patriarch Hui Neng, the principle of sudden enlightenment means that one understands and attains wisdom without going through gradual steps. On this view, understanding is natural and comes to us all of a sudden. This enlightenment is possible because one's mind is purified and void of all desires. By leaving all elements of existence (*dharmas*) as they are, the mind is kept absolutely empty. In sudden enlightenment, one is not attached even to emptiness when one hears about it, nor is one attached to the absence of emptiness. Further, one is not attached to the self when one hears about it, nor is one attached to the absence of the self. One who reaches this level enters the state of *nirvana* without renouncing life and death.

We may ask what would become of a person who achieves sudden enlightenment? At this stage, he is supposed to "rise one more step over the top of the hundred-foot bamboo" as instructed by the *Chan* masters. By doing so, he will fall off and come down on the other side of the bamboo, where he originally set out in search for the enlightenment. He will now do no more than live his daily life and pursue his ordinary activities. Yet, after enlightenment he will view things differently and from a new perspective. What he does is no different from what he did before, but he himself is not the same as he was.

Chinese culture lacks a focus on divinity in a rigid religious sense. Its philosophy and religion are drawn together without a clear boundary between them. The Chinese therefore tend to think about philosophy spiritually and about religion philosophically. In respect to happiness, consideration of philosophy and religion often overlap with a mutual focus on the human condition.

Omniū que sūt dedit in deus sciaz ūar. e gcūnz sūt et inpiūsa didici
Phylosophi si qua ūa dicūnt e fidei nre accomoda sūt abeis ta
e ab inuistis possessoribz in usum nostrum uindicanda.;

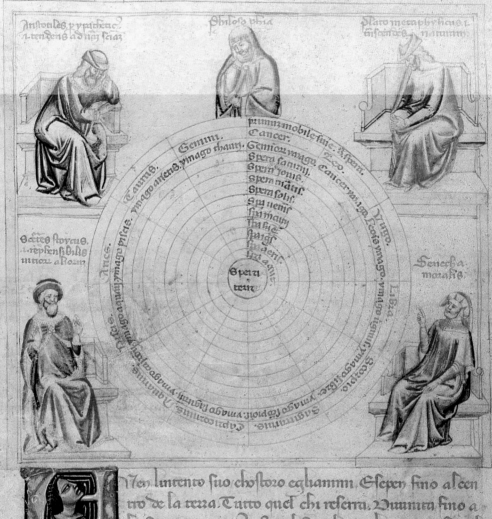

Aristoteles p phisicie
attendens ad nouas sciaz

Philosophia

Plato metaphysicus.
tiscendens... nouarum

Secūndo storcus
a reprehensibilis
mior a Roma

Seneca
moralis

Gemini · Cancer · primū mobile siue Astrū
Taurus · Gemini ymago maurū · Gemiorū maga
Aries · ymago arietis · ymago thaurū · Spera saturni · Cancer...
ymago piscis · ymago anetis · Spera Iouis · Virgo
Spera Martis
Spera solis
Spū neris
Spū mercū · Libra
Spera luna
Spera ignis
Spera aeris
Spera aque
Spera
terre

Saturnus · Capricornus · Aquarius · ymago... ymago figurarū · ymago... Scorpio · ymago Libra

Nen lintento suo chostoro eghianimi. Esepen fino ascen
tro de la terra. Tutto quel chi reserra. Vuuntu fino a
la spieri ottaua. Aristotel spiecchaua. La riente sua ol
tra gliatti inuisibili. per li sensi inuisibili. Cognone e dechiaro no men
che plato Ehe contempia da lato. Phylosophra eghialtri dui magna
nimi che non for pusilanimi. Reprehesen chinulta suo chor sorerra.
Scentes qui sa ferra. Esenecha moral po de li i ehaua. Ehoi bei eho
stumi e saua. Le menti e nectu de ceti nieibili. Ehostoro foro rere
dibili. Vi nostra sede et han quei chel bel prato. Eran de scientia
ornato Pehui phylosophra tutta inpratича. Hauen sū normale
e mathematичaз

4: pleasure, happiness, and the good Stuart McCready

Insights of the Greek philosophers

There can be no end to the troubles of... humanity... till philosophers become kings... or... those we now call kings and rulers really and truly become philosophers... there is no other road to real happiness, either for the society or the individual Plato

From almost any Greek port, a wind or a current will carry your ship to a far-away shore on the Mediterranean. Another will bring you home in a sweeping circle. In the early days of Greek civilization, ships came home laden with trade goods and with Egyptian ideas about art and how to use calculation to give a monument the right shape. They brought back Phoenician ideas about how to preserve speech by drawing sound-imitating characters on a page, and they imported Babylonian ideas about observing the heavens and calculating the speed of the sun in its path across the sky. Their borrowings helped the Greeks establish Western science and a Western philosophy whose ideas about happiness would be almost entirely Greek for more than two thousand years.

Free-thinking Greeks

In the homelands of the ideas the Greeks borrowed, powerful priesthoods kept ideas within proper bounds. Being a priest meant participating in and helping to keep sacred the mysteries that lay at the heart of a civilization. In Egypt, for instance, priest-scribes told artisans exactly where to place their chisels on a piece of stone; this helped to preserve, for three thousand years, an Egyptian style of sculpture that spoke to the gods in the eternal, priestly dialect that the gods understood. And the gods preserved Egypt. In Greece, though, Egyptian-influenced styles, still prominent in the sixth century B.C., gradually gave way to increasingly naturalistic, free-flowing lines, as unregulated sculptors and their patrons explored fleeting moments of earthly beauty. Art was not reserved for other-worldly communication, nor for preserving a bureaucratic and monolithic state.

In the eighth century, the power of the traditional warrior class waned in Greece, and Greek civilization came to rest on the shoulders of small-holding, socially equal farmers. A typical farm was a family concern that owned no more than one or two slaves. The farmers were citizens of more than a thousand independent and quasi-independent towns and city-states. These tiny states were ruled by tyrants (one or a few strong men) or by oligarchies (compacts of powerful families), but these governments were bound to reflect the wishes of ordinary citizens, for the city depended for its existence on the willingness of citizen-farmers to fight together for the tracts of fertile valley-bottom land that neighboring towns wanted.

Cities that felt a common kinship through a shared dialect and shared shrines made alliances. Through trade and control of overseas colonies, or through military dominance of their neighbors, some of them (such as

A seventh-century miniature ivory *kouros* (boy) from Dionysermos. Offerings like this, sometimes larger than life—in stone, bronze, or wood—were left in Greek temples and tombs from about 620 to 480 B.C. During this period they became less solemn and less like similar objects in Egypt and Mesopotamia.

Athens, Sparta, and Thebes) eventually became much more powerful than others. But not until Philip II of Macedon subdued them in 338 B.C. were the Greeks unified under one system of government.

Religion and Greek national myths were defined not by a central priesthood, but by a web of overlapping local traditions and by wandering poets. To build and look after temples and organize religious festivals and religious mysteries, each city-state had its own civic committees and its

Orphic mysteries

Greek religion had its most powerful impact on people's lives through the "mysteries," which were secret rites. Only specially initiated people could attend, but there were many mystery cults—no one who wanted this kind of religious experience was left out, and there were cults to meet almost every variety of personal preference. The ritual provided personal communion with a deity, often when a special image of the deity was dramatically exposed to view after ceremonies that raised the participants' expectations and emotions. The point of keeping the rite secret was to enhance its value—only those who had been suitably purified through initiation ceremonies could come so near to a powerful god without giving offense.

In some of the mysteries, the sense of communion that devotees were seeking was one of mystic ecstasy, especially in extreme forms of the cult of the fertility god Dionysus. The heart of this worship was a secret rite of communion. Ecstasy was variously achieved through alcoholic intoxication, through a frenzied butchering and eating raw of sacrificial animals who represented the god, or—in the early days of this worship—through a similar treatment of a human sacrifice.

In the sixth century in Attica (the region of Greece in which Athens was the most prominent city), a related god, Orpheus, arose within the Dionysian tradition, and attracted a more refined worship. Devotees believed that through asceticism (denying themselves pleasures and comforts), moral purity, and ritual, they could achieve a series of reincarnations in which the divine element present in all humans (and symbolized by Orpheus) would gradually drive out the base and the evil elements. An Orphic funerary tablet of this time congratulates the deceased on entering a new stage in his progression to divinity: "Happy and Blessed One, thou shalt be God instead of mortal!"

In the Orphic mysteries, Dionysus was still worshiped. Meat was still eaten raw as a sacrament, and the rites aimed at ecstasy. But the ecstasy aimed at was spiritual—not a physical intoxication. It was achieved by sheer contemplation of the idea of the divine. Orpheus himself was portrayed as a musician who could play the lyre so well that animals, and even trees and rivers, came to listen to him. He is also portrayed as a seeker after knowledge, one who developed the mind as the most godlike aspect of a human being.

With his sweet music, Orpheus soothes the beasts. This mythical figure was supposed to be a philosopher as well as a musician.

own priestly families. Usually, no one was obliged to believe any specific religious doctrines, and no attempt was made to organize Greek religion into a consistent system of belief.

Poetry was allowed to portray Greek gods squabbling with each other or struggling to control their own passions. These were gods who were subject, like humans, to ill-defined mystical forces such as Fate and Necessity. The national literature that poets created told how the gods dealt with noble figures from a mythical heroic age—based on a time, hundreds of years before, when Greeks had been conquering nomads invading from the north. The morality in the stories concerned obligations that come with leadership and warrior companionship.

There are enduring, universal themes in this literature, largely about the vulnerability of human hopes and desires to the cruelty of Fate. Greek tragedians would eventually make further great literature from them. However, to find religious guidance about how to live ordinary lives in a settled agricultural community or small trading city, people mainly turned to local customs and wise sayings, or they made offerings at local shrines, where oracles would tell their personal fortune.

Babylonian mathematicians and astronomers were priestly oracles. Their meticulous observations of the heavens amount to a devoted search for omens from the gods. They observed, calculated, and predicted, because their king needed to know the future. There was no other role for mathematics or astronomy in Babylon. Greek priests and Greek oracles, however, lacked the power to monopolize ideas about anything, let alone mathematics and astronomy. There was nothing to stop someone from enquiring further if he thought numbers or the heavens were fascinating in themselves. And there was nothing to stop you, if you were so inclined, from asking how you could know for yourself what the world was made of or how you should conduct yourself in it in order to make it a happier place, or at least to make yourself happy.

Every Greek was entitled to his opinion, and because of this opinions were debated, remembered, and commented upon from generation to generation—even ones that the general public thought eccentric and of no practical value. This custom has left us with a remarkable legacy of diverse and conflicting views on subjects that still preoccupy philosophers today.

Inventing philosophy

Early Greek philosophers did not have much to say about happiness, but nevertheless set the stage for later discussions about how we should live. Before they settled down to debates about ethics (the philosophy of right and wrong behavior), Greek thinkers divided into those who were prepared to make sense of the material world and those interested in finding a deeper, truer reality. As these two camps emerged, different outlooks on human happiness emerged with them.

The first philosophers seem to have come from Ionia. This was a strip of coastline across the Aegean Sea in Asia Minor, settled by Greeks in about 1000 B.C. In the sixth century B.C., the city of Miletus produced three famous thinkers. Thales, who was famous for predicting an eclipse (28 May 585 B.C.), was also remembered for the striking claim "everything is from water." He also said that (presumably by analogy with the human soul, seen as that which gives a human body the power to move) a magnet has a soul, for it can move iron particles.

In the following generation, Anaximander regarded the universe as a single, infinite, and divine substance that transforms itself into many appearances and loves symmetry. His younger Miletian contemporary, Anaximenes, thought that the universe consists entirely of air, but packed at different densities to give it different qualities. He argued for this, pointing out that air compressed through pursed lips as it is blown out of the mouth feels cool, and that uncompressed air blown from an open mouth feels warm. From experiments such as these, modern science eventually evolved.

In the same century, the Aegean island of Samos produced a charismatic mystic named Pythagoras who eventually founded a sect in southern Italy based on his own version of the cult of Orpheus. It included a reverence for numbers and a fascination with heavenly bodies. In the fifth century, various thinkers about mathematics and astronomy were called "Pythagoreans," and on this evidence, Pythagoras is sometimes regarded as the father of theoretical mathematics. His mathematics is theoretical because the object of study is mathematics itself, not the practical tasks to which mathematics could be applied. The Pythagoreans were interested in understanding triangularity as an abstraction, whereas Egyptian scribes had been interested in little more than calculating the angles they needed to get right when building pyramids.

Pythagoreans are also supposed to have been the first to combine the Greek words for love ("philo") and knowledge ("sophia") into "philosophy" and to have disdained beliefs that fell short of actually *knowing*. Their model for actually knowing was the certainty with which mathematical truths can be known.

Around 500 B.C., Heraclitus, a philosopher from Ephesus in Ionia, taught that fire was the fundamental substance from which the world is made. He wrote a book of which about a hundred sentences, many of them cryptic, still survive. Other Greeks found his book hard to interpret—his method was apparently to challenge his readers to unravel reality by trying to understand obscure aphorisms, such as "You can't step into the same river twice," which was supposed to help explain his view that "everything is in flux." By the time of Plato and Aristotle, a century later,

Heraclitus was taken to mean that there is no objective world of things to be seen, heard, smelled, tasted, and touched: physical reality is relative— for each of us, the world is just what our own flickering stream of perceptions makes it seem to be.

Heraclitus probably meant something much more difficult and subtle than this. However, the Eleatics (philosophers of the southern Italian city of Elea, who lived at the same time as Heraclitus) *did* dismiss the senses as a source of knowledge about any objective world. The leader of the Eleatics was Parmenides. In a long poem, he argues that whatever really exists must be an unchanging, perfect whole that can be grasped only by the intellect. In one interpretation, he says that the world of changing objects we think we perceive is nothing but a false illusion. An alternative interpretation is that we can justly *believe* in an external world of many changing things revealed by the senses but never *know* this world. The more extreme of these two interpretations, however, is consistent with the strange paradoxes attributed to his follower Zeno. These are meant to show that time, motion, and even the plurality of things, are illusory—an arrow flying through the air, for instance, has to travel half way to its target before it can arrive, but before it can travel half way, it must travel a quarter of the way, and so on to infinity. So there can't be such a thing as arrows flying through the sky, or any bodies moving through space.

Believers in the perceived world were not overwhelmed by these arguments. Not long after Parmenides and Zeno, a Sicilian Greek named Empedocles (c.495–435 B.C.) was developing a new materialism.

A medieval impression of Heraclitus, who thought that all things come from fire.

Completely undeterred by Eleatic arguments, he thought there was a material world, one made up of many different things that changed through time. Earth, air, fire, and water, he said, were the four basic elements from which all other substances were made. Some of the verses he left hint at a theory of the evolution of life that anticipated Charles Darwin's.

Happiness and personality in Greek medicine

Hippocrates (c.460–c.377 B.C.) was the leader of a school of physicians on the Greek island of Cos. His writings were the first to distinguish medical practice from religion on the one hand, and from the unapplied scientific speculations of philosophers on the other. Among the medical principles that guided the Hippocratic school was one that health is affected by four bodily fluids called "humors"—blood, black bile, yellow bile, and phlegm. The humors were related to the four basic elements identified by the materialist Empedocles—fire, earth, air, and water. Fire was related to the blood, and an abundance of it in your bodily system gave you a sanguine temperament (happy and enthusiastic). Earth was related to black bile. An excess gave you a melancholic personality. Too much yellow bile, related to air, made you choleric (irritable), and too much phlegm, related to water, made you phlegmatic (having a slow and stolid temperament). This theory guided physicians through the Middle Ages and into Renaissance times.

The beginnings of ethics

Starting in the fifth century, itinerant teachers—called "sophists" (wise men)—appeared all over the Greek world. They were not usually original thinkers, but instructors in subjects that Greeks wanted to master. For those who could afford it, and especially those wanting to take advantage of expanding opportunities in an increasingly complex society, it became fashionable to be tutored in the learning of the mathematicians and the Ionian materialists, as well as history and geography. Besides the refinement that came with pure learning, though, sophists were usually expected to provide a systematic instruction in the practical arts of persuasion, argument, and politics—the art of getting on successfully in life. This meant they sometimes had to answer questions about ethics.

A particularly well-known sophist was Protagoras (c.490–420 B.C.), from Abdera in Thrace. He is famous for saying that "man is the measure of all things." Regarding ethics, he meant by this that one set of moral beliefs can be true in one community, but not in another. That, he said, is because the rules of correct conduct are a social contract between citizens—they have implicitly agreed to accept them in order that life can be worth living.

A medieval comparison of the four traditional types, with women represented as more likely to be phlegmatic or melancholic (more introverted) and men more likely to be sanguine or choleric (more extroverted). Modern research has not found any pronounced sex difference like this.

GREEK AND MODERN PERSONALITY TYPES COMPARED

Sanguine (happy, hearty) personalities are extroverts. They have emotions but they are stable ones. A phlegmatic personality is typically introverted and stable, while melancholics combine a tendency to be highly emotional with a tendency toward introversion. The choleric personality combines high emotion with extroversion.

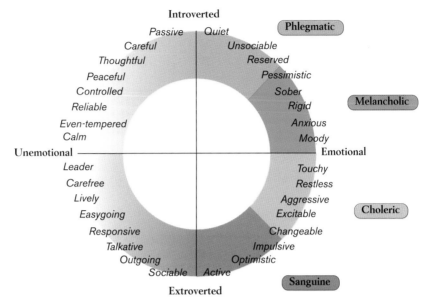

Modern echoes of the four humors

The theory of the humors is the primitive beginning of an understanding that today we express in terms of hormones and neurotransmitters and their chemical effects. As we will see in chapter eleven, modern experimental psychology has found a partial genetic basis for the two most easily measured traits of personality—the degree to which a person is extroverted and the degree to which they are emotional ("neurotic"). A genetic basis suggests that inherited differences in body chemistry are at work.

The four Greek personality types can be translated roughly into modern terms, using these same notions of extroversion and emotionality. The cheerful Greek sanguine type, for example, seems to coincide best with people who are highly extroverted, but with average emotional stability. Some people who are more than averagely extroverted, on the other hand, are also highly emotional. These "choleric" personalities may experience a lot of pleasure but also have to put up with being made unhappy by things that go wrong.

Introverted people with average emotional stability are of the Greek phlegmatic type—not cheerful, but not gloomy. The melancholic type also lacks cheer, but being more emotional is more easily bothered when things go wrong. Like the choleric personality, the melancholic finds it hard to ignore the negative aspects of life.

Many Greeks stuck to the more traditional view that by natural law you just *ought* to worship the gods, honor your parents, and so on. The proof was supposed to be that all cities upheld these principles. Probably a more common sophistical teaching was that by playing by the rules you avoided giving offense and you had a better chance of leading a happy and successful life than an immoderate or overtly impious person could.

These sophistical teachings appealed in one way or another to established convention, and the question arose whether this was strong enough to reign in ambitious men who would want to pursue their own advantage at the expense of the city. This question made people especially anxious, because conventions were crumbling in the fifth century. Economic diversification led to a more urban population in which small-holding land-owners were a less powerful group. In many cities, the old oligarchies of leading land-owning families were displaced, and a struggle ensued between democracy and tyranny.

After leading the Greeks in defeating two Persian invasions early in the century, Athens (already experimenting with democracy) and Sparta (the only city to preserve a traditional warrior caste) emerged as rival powers. Their struggle for dominance, culminating in the twenty-seven year Peloponnesian War (431–404 B.C.) disrupted the Greek world and helped to create unheard of opportunities for the ambitious. Athens, in particular, in relying on naval power, found itself depending on 40,000 landless sailors, to whom it had to extend the franchise. Athenian democracy became unstable and for a time fell back into tyranny.

In 399 B.C., Athenian democracy disgraced itself by trumping up charges of religious impiety against an eccentric seeker after truth called Socrates, and, by a narrow vote, condemning him to death. His real crime seems to have been his habit of challenging people in the street to explain what the conventional wisdom they tried to live by actually amounted to, if anything. One of Socrates' pupils, Plato, was deeply moved by these events. After the execution of Socrates, he renounced the political career he would probably otherwise have pursued, and devoted himself to philosophy. He became convinced that "there is no other road to real happiness, either for society or the individual" except that "philosophers become kings…or…those we now call kings and rulers really and truly become philosophers…"

Which is Socrates and which is Plato?

The Athenian philosopher Socrates (470-399 B.C.) wrote nothing and we know about him only through the accounts of others who knew him at the time. He is the main character in the *The Clouds* (423 B.C.) by the comic playwright Aristophanes, who makes of him several caricatures rolled into one—incorporating everything that had ever been found ridiculous about philosophers, wise men, and other-worldly ascetics.

The Athenian general and military historian Xenophon (c.430–c.355 B.C.) draws a different picture. He portrays Socrates as an ascetic, soldierly traditionalist, who conducted himself with dignity in warfare and walked barefoot through mountain passes. He also says that Socrates never accepted a fee for teaching. Xenophon's account has helped to establish Socrates for all time as the embodiment of personal and intellectual integrity.

Plato (c.428–347 B.C.) was also a pupil. He wrote almost nothing that was not about his teacher. He wrote philosophy as dialogue, and in almost all of his dialogues Socrates is the main character. Since Plato used these writings to explore issues and gradually develop his own views, it is difficult to know when his Socrates is the historical Socrates, when he is Plato putting forward a position he wants us to be convinced of, and when he is instead Plato himself, trying out an idea.

A nineteenth-century impression of how Plato's teacher Socrates might have looked.

Scholars generally agree that, in the earlier dialogues, we can find a picture of Socrates himself. They reveal a man who made a nuisance of himself in Athens by trying to shake his fellow citizens out of their moral complacency. He would stop them in the street and, through step-by-step argument, force them to admit to living by inconsistent, poorly thought-out principles. He did not claim to have very many answers to the questions he posed. His aim was to alert Athenians to the fact that they didn't know as much as they thought they did about how to live. Plato's objective in writing these early dialogues was to stir people to search with him for a way of knowing.

An impression of Plato, c.1475 by van Gent.

The beginnings of hedonism

Plato writes as though Greek ethics began with his teacher Socrates. However, at the same time that Socrates was active in Athens, it seems the materialist philosopher Democritus (c.460–c.370 B.C.) was also exploring ethics. Like Protagoras, he was from Abdera in Thrace. Plato never mentions him, and possibly wasn't aware of him. (Democritus wrote that when he visited Athens, "No one knew me.")

In fact, it is likely that Plato did know of him, but did not deign to speak about him. Democritus was the main figure among the Atomists, who proposed that material things were made up of atoms—minutely small particles of fire, earth, air, and water that could not be divided any further. This was an attempt to answer arguments by the Eleatics to the effect that there couldn't be more than one thing in reality because once you admit that reality can be divided you absurdly admit that reality can be divided again and again unto infinity. Plato thought Parmenides a better philosopher than any of the Atomists, who seemed to him to be arbitrarily concocting a picture of atom-based matter.

The Atomists believed that various skeptical arguments show that you cannot be certain that the material world is as it seems, but they admired Empedocles and agreed that you could at least make sense of what the world seems to be and talk about how it works. Among the points the Sicilian made about the natural world is that living creatures are "naturally directed toward pleasure." It was apparently part of his theory of biology that each different kind of creature is directed towards its specific goals by being so made as to experience pleasure when it achieves them.

Fragments attributed to Democritus make this idea into the earliest identified thesis on hedonistic ethics—the theory that the ultimate goal in life is pleasure. These fragments assert that pleasure is a good: "The mark of things beneficial and harmful is pleasure and unpleasantness," and "A life without celebrations is a long road without an inn." But at the same time, the writer seems to accept that pleasure is not a mark which can be read without rational judgment: "Accept nothing pleasant unless it is beneficial." How this rational hedonism was to work in practice—how we are to distinguish pleasures that are harmful from those which are beneficial—remains unknown.

Socratic hedonism

In one of his early dialogues, the *Protagoras*, Plato presents Socrates, too, as a hedonist. Plato stages an encounter between Protagoras when he was an old man and Socrates when he was young. Socrates challenges the sophist to show how his teaching of social conventions can provide a method for choosing rationally how to behave. Social convention is a hodgepodge of values that have not been reflected upon in any disciplined way, and Socrates argues that the way forward is to adopt a single criterion of value—for instance, pleasure—and then weigh in each case how much pleasure the various available courses of action would bring to us.

The proposal is revolutionary. It would uproot Greeks from what they are accustomed to valuing. But such a hedonism would be a welcome reform in practical reasoning, Socrates argues, because it would make it possible to weigh up every possibility for action on the same scale—how much pleasure it would produce—and elevate practical choice to a level of scientific measurement. The question of why pleasure should be the ultimate criterion, however, is not discussed in the *Protagoras*.

In Plato's dialogue the *Gorgias*, Socrates discusses pleasure with the sophist Callicles. Here he makes it clear that it is not just any pleasure that will do. He claims that a life ruled by reason rather than passion, free as it is from the need to satisfy appetites, is a good one, one that a wise man would choose.

Callicles replies that this principle would make "stones and corpses" into exceptionally happy beings. He asserts instead that the naturally noble and just man will cultivate his appetites and maximize the pleasure he takes in eating, drinking, and sexual indulgence.

The Greeks were devoted revelers. However, Plato was not persuaded that this kind of pleasure had anything to do with a person's good.

Plato's "true happiness"

In most of his dialogues, Plato is not concerned with finding a way to chose the right course of action. What matters instead is choosing the right life. The rest—right behavior on any given occasion—will follow from this. And the right life is distinctly not a life of pleasure, in the ordinary sense.

Plato says that the best life is desirable for its own sake and it is sufficient in itself to satisfy us. But this is not the psychological condition we are so accustomed to identifying with "happiness," for he adds that nothing can be counted as the best life unless it is also what a wise man would prefer to any other. Happiness for Plato has an objective criterion, and *feeling* happy is not good enough.

Socrates persuades Callicles that this view needs rethinking. To have an appetite, he counters, is simply to be dependent on whatever the appetite is for. It is a pleasure to scratch an itch, but that does not mean that having an itch ennobles a person, nor that it would be rational to cultivate itches in order to experience pleasure.

The well-ordered soul

In a later dialogue, the *Republic*, Socrates argues against claims by another sophist, Thrasymachus, that a life of justice is the life of a fool. Thrasymachus maintains that what makes sense is to take advantage of others whenever you can get away with it. Socrates replies that the just man is the man with a well-ordered soul, in which reason is firmly in charge of the emotions and the appetites. As he values only what reason instructs him to value, this man will have no motive to steal from, or otherwise harm, his fellow citizens.

He will feel no need to expropriate from others. His reason will have taught him that managing a need is a more rational way to happiness than being a slave to satisfying the need. Activities that satisfy needs and appetites are pleasant only by comparison with the discomfort that precedes them. They are not intrinsically valuable—they are not "truly pleasant"—because without the discomfort there would be nothing attractive about them.

To recognize true pleasure and the best life, you require the right perspective, Plato believed, and this can be achieved only by a

philosopher—a lover of knowledge. When someone who has the potential to be a philosopher has received the right education—one that liberates the mind from distraction and confusion—then by reason alone he will be able to judge between what is pleasant and unpleasant. Such a person will be in a position to compare the pleasures of the world with the pleasures of pure philosophical contemplation and find the latter more attractive. Philosophical contemplation is not an activity driven by the need to overcome an intermittent pang of need. Rather, it is one done for its own sake. The objects of this kind of pleasure are pure and eternal, unlike the changing, perishable objects that give pleasure in the world. And this kind of pleasure yields an invaluable further reward—truth. So the just life, which is the philosophical life, is its own reward, and it also has rewarding consequences.

The form of the good

Plato's lover of knowledge will be like Parmenides in denying that the buzzing confusion offered to us by the senses represents a knowable reality (and he will be immune to craving after experiences that rely on the senses). Plato was prepared to accept that we can believe in the world of the senses and hold opinions about it, but he did not accept that we could know anything about it. For him, knowledge was restricted to objects comprehended purely by the intellect, such as mathematical truths, and the Forms.

The Forms are ideal paradigms—grasped directly by the intellect—of that which we perceive by way of our senses. For Plato, most people were deluded by the untutored belief that the highest reality is to be found in the imperfect objects encountered in the perceived world. If they were not so deluded, they would recognize that the Form is the reality, and that the many examples of it in the world are imperfect copies. Compared to the Form these copies have as much reality as their own shadows and reflections.

Supreme among the Forms is the Form of the good. Just as the sun makes it possible to perceive the lesser world revealed to us by the senses, the Form of the good illuminates the higher reality that only the mind can grasp. Believing that the world of the senses is the highest reality is like being a prisoner in a cave, taking shadows cast on a wall by a fire to be all that the world has to offer. Becoming a philosopher is like escaping from the cave and coming up into the sunlight to see the world as it really is.

Their knowledge of the good is what qualifies philosophers to discriminate between true and false pleasures, and it is what qualifies them to be kings. It also obligates them. In Plato's ideal republic, philosophers will have to take turns at giving up the pleasures of pure

contemplation in order to go back into the cave to teach and to rule. They will teach the teachable to be philosophers, and so lead them out into the light, where they can achieve their full potential for happiness. They will use their wisdom to legislate in the best interests of the rest, creating a state in which each class achieves a share of such happiness as it is capable of experiencing. Authoritarian rule by these wise, happy thinkers will create the happiest possible society. It will involve the removal of conflict through a number of reforms that shocked most of Plato's readers, such as sharing sexual partners, the abolition of private property, and the creation of equality between women and men.

Just how Plato thought truth would come into the minds of his philosophers was something he did not discuss very much. Dialectic, constructive debate between philosophers, was meant to clear away confusion and make the mind receptive to the light. But actually seeing the light was left as an act of special intuition. Here and there in the dialogues, Plato has Socrates entertain the idea that knowing is equal to remembering eternal truths to which we are exposed while the soul is resting between incarnations. Strong echoes of the old cult of Orpheus, with its program of making humankind more godlike through asceticism and progressive reincarnation, seem to linger in the heart of Plato's philosophical system.

Aristotle's virtuous life

Plato's great pupil, Aristotle (384–322 B.C.) came, at the age of seventeen, from Stagirus in northern Greece to study at Plato's Academy. He stayed for almost twenty years. After Plato died, Aristotle taught in several Greek cities, and tutored the young Alexander the Great, before moving back to Athens in 335 B.C., where he founded his own school, the Lyceum.

Aristotle considered reality to be the material world, which he studied with great interest, developing further the theory of elements proposed by Empedocles. Selecting from and amplifying the work of Greek astronomers and cosmologists, he constructed a picture of an earth-centered universe that (in a form perfected by Ptolemy in about A.D. 140) would go virtually unquestioned throughout the Middle Ages. Similarly, until the Renaissance, he would remain the undisputed authority in physics, biology, logic, and psychology.

Like Plato, Aristotle thought that everything has a unique ideal to which all members of its kind can be compared, but he rejected Plato's theory of Forms. He preferred to speak of every kind having an end toward which it naturally inclines. For example, different types of material, if unimpeded, move to their natural place in the world: stones fall downward toward the center of the earth, where the cold, dry element,

earth, is most at home; flames shoot upward toward a shell of fire Aristotle thought there must be above the atmosphere, where the hot, dry element, fire, is most at home. For many other kinds of thing, the natural end is to fulfill a unique purpose or function. For example, the aim of an axe is to produce efficient chopping, and the aim of a human is to achieve what only a rational animal can: happiness.

Plato taught, and Aristotle accepted, that to be happy a life must be one that is desirable for its own sake, sufficient in itself to satisfy us, and the one that a wise man would prefer to any other. Any organism can feed and grow, and so a life that merely satisfies appetites that enable us to do this is not uniquely human. Humans uniquely are capable of acting in a self-directed way. It is their function to do this, and happiness consists in doing it well.

Living well means living virtuously, where "virtue" is not the moral propriety that the modern world understands but simply the quality of being able to do something well. Human virtue consists in the ability to choose well how to act. This involves a good intellect—knowing how to deliberate wisely. Before learning to deliberate wisely, though, it is necessary to be trained in goodness of character—the ability to overrule passions and appetites as necessary. This amounts in part to selecting the mean between too much of what we are drawn to, and too little of what we are inclined to avoid. For example, courage is the habit of avoiding, to the degree appropriate to the circumstances, both a cowardly concern for one's own safety and a reckless overconfidence. Generosity avoids both extravagance and stinginess. Anger avoids being short-tempered, just as it avoids apathy.

To live the most preferable human life to the maximum—to be happy—it is necessary to have adequate health, material means, friends, associates, and even good luck. You certainly need resources to acquire, for example, the education that teaches virtue, and you will not live a good life if you are struck down by calamities.

Of the activities unique to humans, an outstandingly important one is political life. People of good character and good intellect can fulfill a particularly human function well, and contribute to the general happiness, through active citizenship. This is not done as philosopher kings, but as well-formed individuals living the life of their city. The leaders among them—who will have not only virtue but wealth and friends to help them—have a special opportunity to exercize their virtue, and unlike Plato, Aristotle thought the state that makes the best use of good leaders is a democracy.

But this uniquely human activity is not done for its own sake. Politics and business, says Aristotle, are means to the good things in life, and the best thing in life is leisure, in which we are our own masters. It is the worthy and noble use of leisure time that is the highest form of

happiness. Aristotle could think of no better activity to fill those hours with than the contemplation of science and metaphysics.

Aristotle's description of the happy life begins with the question, what is human nature? If this can be defined, then he believes we will know what aim a human life naturally has, and we will know how to distinguish a good life from a poor one. This starting point has been severely criticized. Saying that humans have an end that belongs uniquely to them implies that we should be able to judge whether or not someone is a good person on the same kind of basis that allows us to judge whether an axe is a good axe. Today, we are more inclined to think of a human life as something that simply happens, like the weather, and the question whether or not someone is a good person is likely to revolve around the impact that person's life is capable of having on others, and unhappy, but kind, people may well be praised for their goodness.

The virtues that Aristotle praises have also been criticized. He paints a picture of generosity, courage, and moderation that is sometimes accused of reflecting not just culture-bound Greek values of his times, but those of the cultivated ruling classes. Because of this, Aristotle's writings need to be sifted carefully to distinguish what is advice for a noble Greek of his day, and what is universal insight into the nature of happiness.

Cynics, Stoics, and Epicureans

While Plato and Aristotle were developing theories that would dominate thinking in the Roman, Christian, Jewish, and Muslim worlds for centuries to come, a number of lesser schools of thought were also making a lasting Greek mark. The Cynics, for example, though known only by their reputation (which was not good), are still remembered for their own way of honoring the legacy of Socrates. They took him to have demonstrated that society has nothing to teach us about how to live, and they drew the further conclusion that the best life is the most natural one. Plato said that Diogenes (404–323 B.C.), the best remembered of them, was "Socrates gone mad."

The name "Cynic" (meaning "like a dog") is derogatory. The life of the Cynics was deemed a dog's life, because Diogenes and others like him (including Crates and his wife Hipparcha, who left a fortune in trust for their children) wandered Greece in poverty without any home. They said they did this because they wanted to rid themselves of vices such as luxury, pride, and malice. Diogenes is supposed to have taught that all that matters is distinguishing virtue from vice. Distinctions between public and private, what's yours and what's mine, citizen, and foreigner are meaningless social conventions that fly in the face of nature. Meeting contempt and giving offense wherever he went, he is said to have been a master of savage repartee.

Zeno (334–262 B.C.), a merchant from Citium in Cyprus, began his philosophical career as a Cynic. He read Xenophon's memoir of Socrates and, impressed, wanted to make contact with the great man's followers. He was introduced to Crates. Zeno embraced the idea that we should follow nature, but he didn't take to the itinerant life. Soon he set up a school in the *stoa poikile* ("painted porch") in Athens.

The Stoics, as the philosophers who met and taught there became known, regarded it as possible, through intellectual discipline, to make themselves invulnerable to misfortune. They also taught that everything that happens is governed by divine providence, and must be for the best. Against Aristotle they held that virtue alone is enough for happiness. Even when calamitous events, or a lack of wealth and good connections, destroy what you are trying to achieve, all that matters is that you acted well. Only if it was your own wickedness that resulted in your children dying in a house fire would you have cause for regret over their loss. Otherwise, the response of the perfectly wise man would be to accept, and be happy with, the life God has given him. The Stoic philosophy eventually found followers in Rome. Marcus Aurelius, emperor from A.D. 121 to 80, wrote a twelve-volume *Meditations*, in which he illustrates how even the great and the powerful can benefit from a philosophy that teaches integrity, acceptance of the inevitable, and understanding toward others.

Epicurus (c.340–c.270 B.C.) was in a rather different vein. He set up a school in Athens in 306 B.C., where he taught atomism and hedonism. He taught that "pleasure is the beginning and the end of living happily." His hedonism was austere, and his followers were not the "epicures" (persons of refined or fastidious taste) his name was eventually lent to, through confusion and misrepresentation. Rather than sensuous pleasure, the Epicureans who followed him mainly sought an absence of pain and

Epicurus taught the pursuit of pleasure and avoidance of pain. Since he regarded most pleasures as ones that result in pain, his followers led an austere life.

anxiety, although the positive enjoyment of friendship was highly valued. Epicureanism spread widely, if always on the fringes. Its chief strategy for avoiding pain and anxiety, and encouraging friendship, was withdrawal into sheltered communities apart from the world. In them, men and women, rich and poor, slaves and freeborn, lived together as equals. Epicurus taught that humans are part of a natural world that exists by a chance coming together of atoms, and he denied any supernatural power is at work in our lives. The Roman Epicurean poet Lucretius (c.95–52 B.C.) wrote:

> *Death is nothing to us, nor concerns us at all,*
> *Since the nature of the soul has been shown mortal.*

He means that there is no reason to fear death, because nothing will happen to us once we are dead. This naturalism in the Epicurean philosophy made it an unsuitable candidate for Christianization when the time came, and it died out during the late Roman empire.

The transition to medieval thought

After the conquests of Alexander the Great, the most important center of Greek learning was the newly founded city of Alexandria in Egypt. It was here that the Jewish philosopher Philo of Alexandria (c.20 B.C.–c. A.D. 50) first put Greek philosophy to work as the handmaid of theology. He synthesized Platonic, Jewish, and Stoic concepts in an account that made nature and human intelligence expressions of divine wisdom. Christians would later put work by Alexandrian Neoplatonists to similar use.

"Neoplatonism" is a term coined by nineteenth-century scholars for a distinctive school of thought that became highly influential in the Roman empire from the third to the fifth centuries A.D. Plotinus (A.D. 204–70), the founder of Neoplatonism, considered himself simply a disciple of Plato. In fact, he brings together ideas from Plato, Aristotle, and the Stoics, and he injects ideas of his own. He introduces, in particular, a supernatural, all-good Ultimate Being, from which all things arise. By this means, the Form of the good becomes God and the rest of the Forms become thoughts in God's mind. Lower beings such as us, living in a lower level of reality such as the material world, share imperfectly in this goodness, and our greatest happiness is to discover and understand this part of ourselves.

Plotinus was an Egyptian who received a Greek education in Alexandria before teaching in Rome, where his disciple Porphyry (c. A.D. 232–304) established Neoplatonism and helped to spread it through the empire. Though Plotinus and Porphyry rejected Christianity, theirs was the philosophical grounding available to Augustine (A.D. 354–430), the Bishop of Hippo in Numidia, when he sat down in the fifth century A.D. to write the first great works of Christian philosophy.

5: the soul and the intellect Sara Sviri

Happiness in medieval philosophy

*And now thither, as to a
pre-ordained place
We are carried by the power
of that bowstring
Which directs what it looses
to a happy mark* Dante

In the Middle Ages, Greek philosophy dominated the Islamic, Christian, and Jewish intellects alike. Aristotelian and Neoplatonic thought harmonized very well with monotheistic religion, and to the contemplative mind offered a vision of happiness as an attractively *intellectual* attainment. For medieval philosophers, this also meant a contemplative state bound up with the knowledge of celestial intelligences that inhabited the farther reaches of the spiritual universe.

Overflowing divinity

In order to get a closer look at the medieval understanding of the nature of happiness, let us visualize a universe made of rotating, luminous spheres. According to the Ptolemaic astronomical structure, which reigned supreme from the second right through the fifteenth century and even beyond, Earth stood at the center of nine concentric spheres, or "heavens."

Following in the footsteps of Dante (1265–1321) and other contemplative pilgrims—traveling not by means of a spaceship, but by means of a penetrating, imaginative mind—we set out on a journey that starts off from Earth, the lowest region in this cosmological structure, and then make our way upwards into the increasingly loftier, subtler, and more brilliant spheres of the seven stars and planets: the moon, Mercury, Venus, the sun, Mars, Jupiter, and Saturn. We could then, perhaps, journey through the eighth sphere of the Fixed Stars, to the ninth, the All-Encompassing sphere, and, finally, beyond time and space, to the point where all journeys end, to the Realm of the Divine Being.

There, contemplating God's mind in Its dazzling brilliance, we would attain true and ultimate happiness. Our state of felicity (Greek *eudaimonia*) would result from the understanding of the divine radiance from which—as from an immense source of light—all that is derives its life and existence. With the few individuals who had reached this state, we would then understand the nature of existence as an overflow that emanates, radiates, from the unfathomable divine source. This overflow, as it moves away from its source, produces a creative chain reaction in which luminous entities—intellects, souls, and spheres—emerge in a descending order. All these entities have their own light and power, but the more remote they are from the source, the darker and weaker they become. Eventually, as the process of emanation slows and comes to a halt, our own world, Earth, comes into being.

A lucid description of the hierarchical, life-engendering concept of the divine "overflow" is offered by the twelfth-century Jewish philosopher Moses Maimonides. In his seminal work, *The Guide of the Perplexed*, written in Egypt and originally in Arabic, he writes:

It is further to show that governance overflows from the deity, may He be exalted, to the intellects according to their rank; that from the benefits received by the intellects, good things and light overflow to the bodies of the spheres; and that from the spheres… forces and good things overflow to this body subject to generation and corruption… For the overflow coming from Him, may He be exalted, for the bringing into being of separate intellects, overflows likewise from these intellects, so that one of them brings another one into being…

The twelfth-century Jewish philosopher Moses Maimonides, who wrote that "the perfection of man… is apprehension of God…" and that, "The way of life of such an individual, after he has achieved this apprehension, will always have in view loving-kindness, righteousness, and judgment, through assimilation to His actions."

Dante's vision of Paradise

In the *Divine Comedy*, Beatrice explains to the Italian poet Dante the nature of Paradise—that "celestial sphere" at which he has arrived in his visionary journey.
She says:

> *...Everything that is created*
> *Is part of a mutual order, and that is the shape*
> *which makes the universe resemble God...*

> *Here the superior beings see the traces*
> *Of the eternal power, which is the end*
> *For which the rule I have spoken of was made...*

Dante and Beatrice, at the end of their journey, ascend from Saturn to the heaven of the Fixed Stars. Approaching heaven through the rings of light, they look down on the sun in its chariot.

The providence which sets all this in order
With its light gives quiet to the heaven
In which there turns the fastest sphere of all;

And now thither, as to a pre-ordained place,
We are carried by the power of that bowstring
Which directs what it looses to a happy mark.

Cosmic angels

Contemplating the overflow emanating from God, the Fountain of Life, religious medieval philosophers were inspired by feelings of love and awe. The philosophers maintained that movement—on any level of the structure of the universe—was always generated by a passionate love for that which is higher, loftier, subtler, wiser, and more beautiful. Just as a human being's progress towards perfection and happiness was seen to be propelled by the desire to contemplate God and the celestial beings in order to imitate them, so also the movement of the celestial beings themselves was generated by an attraction to assimilate with the next rung on the ascending ladder of Being—and so on.

The multi-layered universe was conceived of as a *conscious*, desirous, moving whole, and the spheres that rotated in it in perpetual motion were figured as living, conscious entities pulled upwards by their innate desire to become more perfect and more Godlike. In principle, then, two polar movements were envisioned as propelling the universe: an overflowing life-engendering movement which, as it creates, proceeds from the uppermost downward, and a perfection-aspiring movement that perpetually aims upward.

The vision of a conscious, love-driven universe was associated with another insight, that the universe possesses both an intellect and a soul, or, rather, several intellects and souls. Each sphere was believed to possess a "soul" (in Greek, *psyche*) as its principle of "movement," and an "intellect" (in Greek, *nous*) as the principle of consciousness and order. The two principles were intrinsically connected, since without consciousness and contemplation, the movement of the "soul" could not be envisaged. Alongside the hierarchy of spheres, the medieval philosopher postulated yet another idea: that of the so-called "separate intellects."

The lowest in the hierarchy of intellects, and the one most directly connected with our earthly abode, was known as the Active Intellect. For those who were more familiar with scriptural language, these "intellects" were sometimes identified with the angels.

An angel sets to the task of generating movement in the heavenly spheres (after a medieval illustration).

The fountain of life, as depicted in a manuscript of the early ninth century.

Above and below the moon

Medieval systems—whether cosmological, spiritual, social, anthropological, or biological—were fundamentally hierarchical. The spheres were seen as being put in motion by a series of instigators, one higher and more powerful than the other, and man was also seen as a complex governed by lower (physical), as well as higher (spiritual), functions. As above so below; or, to put it in an idiom frequently employed by medieval philosophers: the universe was seen as a *macrocosmos* whose laws and structures were reflected in the *microcosmos*, namely, in the human being.

Ibn Rushd (Averroes), the thirteenth-century Muslim philosopher from Andalusia, receiving acclaim.

All human beings were seen as citizens of two worlds: the sublunar (below the moon) world of nature and matter and the supralunar (above the moon) world of spiritual souls and intellects. Human beings, as all things made of "matter" (the different compounds of the four elements) in this sublunar region called Earth, were subject to the law of "generation and corruption," that is to say, growth and decay, life and death. As far as the human body was concerned, its existence as a physical, material entity was short and transient: when its time came, it simply perished.

But human beings were more than just matter. Loftier faculties were also part of their make-up. These faculties resembled the beings of the celestial realms: the "soul," with its internal senses of memory, imagination, and awareness; and the "intellect," the regulating, discriminating principle of cognition and order. These higher faculties, it was believed—with the right disposition and after rigorous training—might overcome the laws of nature and survive the decay of the body. Since, in essence, the soul and the intellect were non-corporeal, they did not necessarily perish when physical death occurred.

Happy conjunctions

The intellect, sometimes called "the rational faculty" was the highest asset with which the human being was endowed. This is why, ever since Aristotle, a human being was defined as a "rational animal"; animal, as she or he was part of the animalistic aspect of the physical world. But also "rational"—an attribute that pointed at other, metaphysical possibilities of bliss, perfection, and perpetuity.

It is here that the cosmological and the anthropological (or human-based) systems converge. The visionary, contemplative journeys to the realms beyond Earth—journeys which nurtured European culture far beyond the Middle Ages—could not be envisaged were it not for the understanding that a meeting between the human and the supra-human intellect was possible. Such a meeting was referred to in the philosophical vocabulary as "conjunction." The human intellect, itself sparked off from higher realms, could, if it so aspired, conjoin with the divine intellect. It is this conjunction which brought about happiness.

"For you see," writes Ibn Rushd (1128–1198) (in Latin, Averroes), the thirteenth-century Muslim philosopher from Andalusia, "all philosophers agree that the ultimate felicity of man is in his apprehension of the separate intellects." And Ibn Bajja (in Latin, Avempace), Ibn Rushd's twelfth-century compatriot and co-religionist, wrote:

> By corporeality man is an existing [temporal] being; by spirituality he is a more noble being; and by intellectuality he is a divine and virtuous being...When he reaches the ultimate end, when he has an intellection of the simple substantial intellects...he becomes one of those intellects...

Medieval philosophers, such as al-Farabi, Ibn Sina (otherwise known as Avicenna), Maimonides, and Thomas Aquinas, debated whether this felicitous conjunction could be achieved by human beings while still within their physical bodies. Most doubted, or even denied, that this was possible; some, however, strongly believed it was. When the powerful faculty of imagination joined forces with the contemplative mind, they argued, and when this took place in total detachment from the physical senses and functions, then a prophetic-like, blissful conjunction could take place even during one's lifetime. One could then contemplate the heavenly spheres, or even the formless Glory of God, in a state of pure, timeless, spiritual bliss. Without doubt, Dante's journey and its poetic testimony derive from the certitude that such a possibility is available for the higher faculties of man.

Coming down to earth

It was the contemplation of God (in Greek, *theoria*) and the Supernal Intellects, which, for medieval philosophers, constituted ultimate happiness. God—the Prime Cause, the Unmoved Mover, the still point at the center of a rotating universe—was the object of love and aspiration for the human soul and intellect as well as for the souls and intellects of all higher entities.

In the endeavor "to resemble God," the contemplative who reached the felicitous state of conjunction was called upon to make one more—rather surprising—step: to come *down* to earth again in order to impart, teach, lead, and, more importantly, practice in life those divine principles which he had apprehended in theory in the detached states of consciousness. Like Plato's liberated cave dwellers, their duty once they had seen the sun was to return to their brothers who were still in darkness and help them to escape from ignorance into a love of knowledge. This idea culminates in Maimonides' intriguing vision of human perfection expounded in *The Guide of the Perplexed*. In the aspiration to "imitate God," he suggests, the contemplative, by means of practical activity, should make manifest in the world the divine attributes of loving-kindness, righteousness, and judgement, alluded to by the Prophet Jeremiah (9:23). This is the ultimate perfection leading to true happiness. Maimonides writes:

> It is clear that the perfection of man…is the one acquired by him who has achieved…apprehension of God, may He be exalted, and who knows [that] His providence extend[s] over His creatures as manifested in the act of bringing them into being and in their governance…The way of life of such an individual, after he has achieved this apprehension, will always have in view loving-kindness, righteousness, and judgement; through assimilation to His actions, may He be exalted, just as we have explained several times in this treatise.

When they came down to earth, however, philosophers found that there were many for whom happiness was not an intellectual, but a more direct experience. Among these were the Jewish, Islamic, and Christian mystics of the next three chapters.

6: the Kabbalah and Hasidism Naftali Loewenthal

Happiness in Jewish mysticism

God is good and sends me all I need—I have never known suffering at all Rabbi Zusya

The term Kabbalah ("received tradition") refers to a vast body of Jewish mystical thought reflecting the Bible, the Talmud, Jewish practice, and, above all, life itself. The roots of this tradition go back to prophetic teachings and Temple times, but many of the works expounding its ideas were written in the Middle Ages.

Mystical tradition

In thirteenth-century Spain, there were small groups of mystics studying the Kabbalah. In the sixteenth century, the town of Safed in Northern Israel was a major center. In the eighteenth century, the eastern European Hasidic movement, founded by Rabbi Israel Baal Shem Tov (who died in 1760) broadened the study of the mystical tradition so that certain aspects of it became part of daily life for general Jewish society. This process has continued and increased in contemporary times. The Habad-Lubavitch Hasidic group, in particular, has tried to make Jewish mystical teachings accessible to everyone.

The Kabbalah presents information about the spiritual realms which are the background to the visible world. The first level of happiness is knowledge: if you know what is happening and why, you are far less likely to be anxious about it. The Kabbalah also explains techniques of thought and of action, leading to mystical or spiritual experiences, which include ecstasy, mystical joy, and the excitement of spiritual discovery.

Some forms of mysticism tend to leave the world behind, searching for holiness on a remote spiritual plane; Jewish mysticism in general, and particularly Hasidism, seeks to discover the holiness implicit *in* the world. The effect is that religious observances such as prayer, study of sacred texts, fulfilment of the Commandments (for example, helping other people), together with seemingly earthly activities including eating, making love within marriage, going for a walk, working at one's job, and simply *being*, all become modes of experiencing intense spiritual joy. The worldly physical experience becomes so imbued with the spiritual that it is at the same time an inspiring communion with the Divine.

Exile from Eden

A core idea from the Jewish mystical tradition, in terms of the quest for happiness, is the story of Adam and Eve in the Garden of Eden. Together with them was the Divine Presence. The world itself expressed holiness. For Adam and Eve, every moment of being was joy and harmony. They were happy in an ultimate and total sense. They were together with the Divine.

This expresses what human life *could* be like. We could be physical human beings, men and women, engaging in physical activities. Yet our lives could express holiness in every detail. This is the goal. However, as everyone knows, Adam and Eve committed an error: they ate from a tree that they had been told to avoid. In other words, there was a border they were forbidden to cross—but they crossed it. The effect was that the Divine Presence departed from the world—that is, it became hidden. According to the Kabbalah, this is the effect of sin and of evil—the concealment of the Divine, from the individual and from others, and from existence itself.

The creation of Adam and Eve, from the Golden Haggadah, a fourteenth-century Hebrew manuscript.

Concealment and revelation

The concealment of the Divine caused by the error in the Garden of Eden means that the world now is full of pain. The goal of human life is to reverse this process: to bring the Divine back into the world, and restore the state of harmony and joy. A key step in this process was the divine revelation at Mount Sinai.

The Zohar, source book of the Kabbalah, says that at Mount Sinai the Divine was revealed, not just from the mountain, but from everywhere. Overt holiness had returned to existence. The Talmud says any who were ill were cured; the blind could see. There was a possibility of harmony and joy for all time.

At Mount Sinai there was a revelation of Divine Law: the Ten Commandments. This was a revelation of Divine intimacy. Humanity and God could again connect together, in a world of human reality.

The practical manifestation of this was the construction of the Sanctuary (described in Exodus, chapters 25–27), the prototype of the Temple in Jerusalem. This functions as a continuation of the Mount Sinai atmosphere. The Divine Presence was again revealed in the world, this time in the Holy of Holies.

As is clear from the Bible and from history, this was not the end of the story. There were many ups and downs to come. As explained by the Jewish mystics, each step was a stage leading towards an ultimate goal, when the Divine Presence will be revealed not only in the Holy of Holies in the Temple, but also in the heart of each person.

Then the spiritual intimacy of the Garden of Eden will be regained. At this point, the Divine Law will be kept naturally. People will want to follow the Divine teaching just as they want to breathe. The world will be a physical world, yet it will at the same time reveal its inner essence as a dwelling for the Divine. There will be ultimate joy, true and eternal happiness.

The happiness of the individual

Does this mean that all happiness is deferred to the future? Not at all. Every moment of life is an opportunity to make a step towards the ultimate joy—and also to experience it on the way.

In kabbalistic texts, the Divine is conceived as "the Infinite," beyond all description or definition, and also beyond all Names. This is the ultimate, unknowable essence of the Divine, utterly beyond existence. Yet there is also a "lower" realm of Divine spirituality, described in terms of Ten Divine Manifestations (*Sefirot*).

The state of Exile described above is defined by the kabbalists as a state of disunity among the Divine *Sefirot*. However, each individual has the power to bring about a "union" within the spiritual realms. Each man and woman can help achieve *Tikkun*, the "repair" of the spiritual dimension of existence through the process of daily life, lived in observance of the teachings of the Law, including its spiritual components such as the command to love God (Deuteronomy 6:5, 11:1, 13). In the details of our lives, each person has the power to bring about a spiritual unification, which is part of the process of bringing *Tikkun* and Redemption to the world. This sense of cosmic meaning to ordinary daily activities is a central path to happiness.

Personal redemption

This ultimate goal is in the future, yet the steps towards it are in the present. This can achieve what the Hasidim describe as the "personal Redemption." For the individual personally, now, it is as if in some ways the Redemption has been attained.

One example of this process is escape from the trap of one's own ego. The ego conceals our inner, spiritual reality. It makes us selfish and self-indulgent. This is personal exile. Redemption means freedom from the prison of one's own self. This is an important form of happiness.

The idea that each person is involved in a cosmic process leading to the revelation of the Divine in the world gives meaning to the ups and downs of life. A basic principle is that everything we encounter is guided by God, including anything we see as bad and depressing. It is a challenge to which we have to respond in the best way, to overcome or to transform. Hasidic teachings do not recommend being passive, but they do tell us that the greater the difficulty, the more intimate the relationship with God. This leads to the Jewish ideal of finding joy in suffering.

The disciples of the Hasidic leader Rabbi Dov Ber (d.1772) were discussing the Talmudic statement that one should accept suffering with joy. "How is this possible?" they asked. Rabbi Dov Ber advised them to visit another of his disciples, Rabbi Zusya, who lived some distance away. He would explain to them how to accept suffering with joy.

The disciples were pleased with this advice. All knew that Rabbi Zusya lived a life of poverty, illness, and suffering. He would surely be able to explain.

When they reached the hovel in which he lived he jumped up with joy to greet them. They explained why they had come: "Our teacher told us to enquire from you how to accept suffering with joy."

Rabbi Zusya looked puzzled. "Why did he send you to *me*?" he asked. "God is good and sends me all I need—I have never known suffering at all. So how can I help you?" Why did he not know of suffering? Perhaps because he saw through the disguise of everyday existence: he perceived the Divine goodness within.

The joy of contemplation

To perceive Divine goodness is a constant goal. How does one achieve this form of sight? One answer is, through spiritual practices such as contemplation. The contemplative learns to see the Divine inner reality in all things: he or she discovers the holiness implicit in existence. Hasidic texts such as *Tanya* by Rabbi Shneur Zalman of Liadi (c.1800) seek to guide the person in this journey, which can lead to truly ecstatic experience.

This is expressed particularly in Hasidic prayer. During prayer the person enters another realm of consciousness and delight. For example, he or she might think about the stream of Divine energy which is flowing through all existence. This spiritual energy is the inner reality of everything. Whether a leaf or a stone or a piece of furniture in the room: its true being is Godliness. In Hebrew, words have numerical values (called Gematria). The Hebrew word for Nature has the same numerical value as one of the names for God.

Ecstasy through action

Perceiving oneness in existence can lead us toward harmony and joy. Meditating on this idea, seeing all kinds of different aspects and expressions of it, can lead to ecstasy.

However, the Hasidim ask: is this ecstasy real? How can one make such mystical, other-worldly perceptions about one's own living reality? An interesting answer is given: through action. Action, the Hasidic sages tell us, is at the very lowest level of one's being. It is lower than thought, intellect, and feeling. Since it is the lowest level, it can function like a "lever," applied at the lowest point of a system, to elevate the whole. This means, simply put, that the path of the good action elevates one's entire being, bringing genuine happiness for oneself and others.

Action is the point where one often confronts a choice. Someone needs our help. Can we be bothered to *act*? The Hasidim teach that each act of goodness and kindness helps bring Redemption to the world.

What if one has done wrong? What if there have been bad actions, causing pain and harm? Or bad words, or even just bad thoughts?

Rabbi Shneur Zalman of Liadi (1745–1812), expressed the joy of contemplation in texts such as his *Tanya*. He was known by a painting made of him when he was arrested by the Czar in 1800, on false charges which were later dismissed.

The joy of repentance

Built firmly into the mystical system of Judaism is the theme of repentance, which is always possible. In the process of repentance the person joins the Divine on a level beyond transgression. Sin produces a stain on the soul, and causes harm in spiritual realms. Yet reaching a new intimacy with God, through the power of repentance, brings about unity. This causes a healing radiance to flow, purifying the person's soul, enabling one to reach new spiritual heights. The idea that one can reach such spiritual heights that sin is forgiven is the basis of the Jewish day of atonement (Yom Kippur). Yet this process applies every day. The essential step is the *decision* that one is not going to fall into the trap again. The step of repentance is joyful. Living up to the decision to improve brings happiness.

The family

The happiness of the individual is multiplied when he or she becomes not just one individual, but a husband or wife and founds a family. Jewish spiritual teachings present the family, for all nations, as a path to fulfilled joy. These teachings advise people to respect basic rules of modesty, to have wholesome, faithful marriages, and to look forward to bearing many children.

Friday night, the sacred Sabbath, embodies the concept of happiness in a traditional Jewish home. The wife and daughters, demurely yet beautifully clothed, light the Sabbath candles. The Zohar says that through this they bring peace into the world. The husband makes a blessing on a goblet of wine and shares it with his wife, with their children, and with the guests at the table. The special Sabbath bread is eaten with a delicious meal.

Spiritual teachings and stories are related, and there is singing of special melodies. The Divine Presence is in the home. At this moment above, in the spiritual realms, and below, in the human realm, there is unity.

The idea of family is very important to the Jewish way of life, so the Sabbath meal is a time for the whole family to get together.

The sacred union

At night, the husband and wife are together. Their union is sacred. Together, they enter a Divine realm, partaking of joy and of holiness. Because this physical union is so holy, there are laws regulating when it takes place. The wife attends a ritual pool a week after her period ends. Each month she becomes like a new bride, a virgin.

The Hebrew words for "man" and "woman," when joined together, include the Divine Name. The married couple know that the Divine Presence is with them in their home and in the most intimate aspect of their lives together. They would be happy to be blessed with yet another child. Yet even when this is unlikely, for whatever reason, their union is sacred and draws holiness into the world.

Symbolizing this joy, in a most public way, is a traditional Hasidic wedding. Men dance with men and women dance with women, with a curtain of modesty between them. Yet, the joy is immense. The Talmud tells of sages dancing and juggling at weddings 1,500 years ago, and the tradition still continues. The great joy is because the Divine Presence is being revealed in this human plane of existence.

Below left and right: Men and women dancing separately at a joyful Hasidic wedding.

אִישׁ (iYsh) man

אִשָּׁה (ishAH) woman

Right: The Divine Presence is expressed in marriage with Hebrew words (with pronunciation) for man and woman. When joined, these include the Divine Name, which is sacred to Jewish belief and therefore cannot be reproduced in full here.

י--ה (Y--AH) Divine Name

Contemplatives in a Habad synagogue. As Rabbi Zalman also showed, joy can come through quiet connection with the Divine.

Joy depends on the individual

The Jewish mystics tell us to strive for joy. The great sixteenth-century kabbalist Rabbi Isaac Luria emphasized the need for joy, at every step of life. He gave a new twist to the Biblical verse which says that suffering and exile come "because you did not serve God with joy and a good heart, when you had everything" (Deuteronomy 28:47). "You may have served God," said Rabbi Isaac, "but you did not serve God *with joy*. Had you been joyful, there would never have been Exile."

The Hasidim explain why. Through joy, the person will find it easier to reveal the Divine. Rabbi Shneur Zalman gives the example of two wrestlers struggling together. The one who is more joyful and is quicker on his feet will win, rather than the one who is stronger. In the same way joy will aid each person in his or her continuous spiritual struggle to do good.

Of course, sometimes this is supremely difficult. People feel deeply depressed and can see no good in themselves or the situation. Rabbi Nachman of Braslav (c.1800) advised that we should try to find "one good point." On this basis one can go forward. A contemporary Hasidic leader, Rabbi Menachem Schneerson (who died in 1994), advised: "Think good—and *it will be good!*"

Happiness is making others happy

There is a story in the Talmud that someone wanted to be told the whole of Jewish teaching, while he stood on one foot. He was told by a famous first-century Rabbi named Hillel: whatever would make you unhappy, do not do to anyone else. Hillel said that is the whole of Jewish teaching, the rest is commentary.

The Jewish mystics often quote this story. The kabbalistic prayer book begins with the words: "I hereby accept on myself the positive command: Love your neighbor as yourself." From the Jewish point of view, one can best find happiness by making others happy.

For the kabbalists and Hasidic teachers, happiness is not only a reward that is granted from God to us. It is part of our human effort, trying to live up to the spiritual ideal that human happiness and joy are not the end of the path, they are the beginning.

Think good—and it will be good!

Rabbi Menachem Schneerson

7: living in the moment Sara Sviri

The alchemy of happiness in Sufism

His end will return to his beginning, and he [will] be as he was before he was Al-Junayd

Since the eighth century, mysticism in Islam has been connected with Sufism, so named because of the wool (*suf*) from which wandering ascetics made their garments. Influenced by Christian asceticism and other mystical systems, they took inspiration from Koranic verses that emphasized God's all-pervading mercy and his intimate, timeless relation to his creatures.

Sufism and Islam

The focus of Sufism is on psychological and spiritual attainment during one's lifetime rather than on the reward or punishment that one's actions will incur in the afterlife. The concept of happiness (*sa'ada*) in orthodox Islam, by contrast, stems from the Koranic vision of devout believers—named "happy"—attaining eternal bliss after death—"they shall be in Paradise." Those who have erred and sinned in this world are named "wretched" and in the world to come "they shall be in the Fire [of Hell]" (11:105–108). It was not until early in the twelfth century that mainstream Islam reconciled the mystic revelations of Sufism with traditional precepts of creed and practice.

"The Sufi is the child of his time," goes a well-known dictum. This does not mean fitting in with the spirit of the times, but living in the moment. This is not living hedonistically *for* the moment, but being fully committed—wholeheartedly and with no reservations—to a search for the essence and core of one's being.

"Time," in Sufi terminology, means "moment"; in fact, it means a timeless moment, a sacred present, a moment that is not defined by the linear flow of minutes, days, or years along the past–future axis of our ordinary conception of time. Seeking the promised happiness in the world to come suggests a futuristic outlook—for mystics a second-best kind of happiness. They have always been prepared to give it up for the pursuit of true "happiness"—the happiness that emanates from being at one with God, with Allah—the highest principle of Being, known in the Sufi tradition also by the divine name "the True" or "the Real" (*al-Haqq*). The thrust of the Sufi's quest is to attain this happiness during his or her lifetime and when still in the earthly body. Nevertheless, the Sufi's attention is placed in what lies *beyond* the boundaries of terrestrial life and the physical body. The following ecstatic verses, written by Jalal al-din Rumi—one of the greatest Sufi poets of the thirteenth century—mirror the vision that sees in mystical "oneness" the highest point of fulfillment and happiness that can be attained in life:

> *I have put duality away, I have seen that the two worlds are one;*
> *One I speak, One I know, One I see, One I call.*
> *He is the First, He is the Last, He is the Outward, He is*
> *the Inward;*
> *If once in this world I win a moment with thee,*
> *I will trample on both worlds, I will dance in triumph forever.*
> *O Shamsi Tabriz, I am so drunken in this world*
> *That except of drunkenness and revelry I have no tale to tell.*

Whirling Dervishes. Dervishes are Sufist monks. Some seek ecstasy by performing a whirling dance.

The awakening

The pursuit of happiness in Sufism is a transformative, alchemical process. At some point—either at one of life's major crossroads, or after suffering a heartbreaking loss, or as a result of an inspiring encounter, or for no apparent reason—an "awakening" takes place in a man's or a woman's consciousness. Sufis refer to this awakening as conversion, or "the turning of the heart."

This awakening is a shattering event of transformative intensity. In its wake all previous routines and perspectives lose their familiar appeal. Life is turned upside down. A man or a woman comes to realize that the life they have lived so far—with its pursuit of physical, material, emotional, mental, and even religious gains—lacks any sense of real purpose and has no substantial, true meaning. In the language of the Sufis, one is then overpowered by an intense longing for fulfillment of a kind that, based on previous experiences and notions, his or her mind cannot conceptualize or refer to. This "longing" stands at the root of the Sufi mystical experience. For Rumi, quoted above, the meeting with a wandering Dervish named Shamsi Tabriz in the market of the Turkish town of Konya was such a heart-turning event. When such longing is awakened, a search begins, a quest for the everlasting source of happiness.

With the "awakening" also comes flashes of a strange kind of remembering: a "memory" is stirred up from the depths of one's being of a long-forgotten intimacy and union with a divine beloved. This memory, however, cannot trace any event or any entity along one's personal chronology. It defies one's ordinary sense of time. It carries with it the flavor of a primordial moment before time, before creation, when the souls of all human beings were held within the embrace of the One, the Real, with no differentiation, without boundaries. This memory of the soul, too, lies at the roots of the Sufi tradition. It is nourished by a Koranic verse which outlines the primordial relationship between mankind and God:

> *And when thy Lord took from the children of Adam, from their loins, their seed, and made them testify touching themselves, "Am I not your Lord?" They said, "Yes, we testify." (7:172.)*

The day of the covenant

For Sufis, the vision that reverberates through this verse is both universal and personal, collective and individual. This primordial moment in the prehistory of every human soul is known in the Sufi tradition as "the Day of the Covenant." In this covenant, a relationship is established between God and mankind, a relationship that is built upon two polar focal points: at one end the witnessing and testimony of God's absolute Lordship—and

A caravan of pilgrims on the road to Mecca.

hence of mankind's total servanthood; and on the other the experience of God's nearness and intimacy. For Sufis, a fundamental confirmation of this nearness is the Koranic verse, "I am nearer to you than your jugular vein" (50:16). Sufi mystical knowledge is the realization that emerges from contemplating and living the message that these verses convey: saying an unconditional "Yes" to God's sovereignty—and carrying consciously the memory of God's nearness.

Al-Junayd, the master of the ninth-century Sufi circle in Baghdad (probably the first circle of mystics named Sufis), writes:

> *"In this verse, God tells you that He spoke to them at a time when they did not exist, except so far as they existed in Him. This existence is not the same type of existence as is usually attributed to God's creatures; it is a type of existence which only God knows...Embracing them, he sees them in the beginning when they are non-existent and unaware of their future existence in the world. The existence of these is timeless."*

Returning home

Once on the full-blown mystical path, all that unfolds in life bears for the Sufi the stamp of the primordial moment, the "Day of the Convenant." Life's goal, after this realization, becomes simply this: to return to the very beginning, to the dawn of existence, to the Source of Being—to return *home*. The goal and purpose of the mystic—that which constitutes his and her true happiness—is to return to the state in which they were before they were created. Al-Junayd expounds this idea in the following classic passage:

> *"What is the unity of the mystic? That he be as a lifeless body in front of God...in a state of annihilation from his self and from people's expectations..., devoid of sense-perception and bodily movement, so that Truth may fulfill what It had willed for him, namely: that his end will return to his beginning, and that he be as he was before he was... Unity means to come out of the confinement of temporality into the spaciousness and the expanses of timelessness."*

Junayd is alluding here to mystical states that the soul experiences while still within the living body. Fulfillment, happiness, felicity—all these are names for an experience of a mystical union, an oceanic experience, in which the personal "I," the individual self, merges or drowns within the all-encompassing benevolent Being of the One.

But these moments of elated merging are far from frequent. More often than not, what the seeker experiences is separation. The seeker's ardent love and longing often seem one-sided and unrequited. The lover yearns, but where is the Beloved? For a very long time, the soul may go through the burning pain of longing without any fulfillment. It traverses valleys of unspeakable loneliness and despair, and in this process, it learns how to wait. The waiting hones the soul, polishes it, cooks it, and prepares it for the moments of union. This is the alchemical aspect of a transformation that makes the soul ready for the longed-for nearness and union. "I was raw," says Rumi, "then I was cooked, then I was eaten."

Mystical love, say the Sufi masters, appears one-sided and unreciprocated because the soul is covered by many veils. There may be an initial, fleeting recognition that awakens the heart and sets it ablaze, but from then on, for most of the time, the path to the beloved goes through an existential wilderness, filled with different kinds of effort and pain. But slowly, when the hardship of the journey is endured, the veils are lifted and the soul begins to take in the expanding vistas of that *other* landscape for which it longs.

The inner journey

This quest for mystical happiness has been profusely recorded in Sufi manuals and in Sufi poetry and fables. One of the most poignant descriptions of the inner journey has been given by Farid ad-Din Attar, a Persian poet of the twelfth century. In an epic poem titled *The Conference of the Birds*, he describes the journey of the birds who go in search of their king, the fabulous Simorgh. The different kinds of birds, symbolizing different human types, go through seven harrowing valleys. Most perish, but a few persevere during the hardship and trials to reach the king's court. There, the mystery of Being and Oneness is revealed to them.

Sufism's rich and idiosyncratic vocabulary, mostly in Arabic and Persian, refers to two avenues leading to the sought-for inner transformation: the "stages" and "stations" (*maqamat*), which outline the "horizontal," effortful direction, and the "states" (*ahwal*), which mark the ecstatic, ephemeral yet timeless mystical experiences. The *maqamat* (singular *maqam*) have an ascetical flavor. They denote the relentless struggle against psychological—as well as metaphysical—obstacles and deterrents (for example, Satan, alias *Iblis*) which the mystic must encounter on the path. The *ahwal*, on the other hand, bear the sweet, rapturous taste of a divinely bestowed ecstatic experience that "flashes like lightning" and then recedes, leaving behind it an intense emotional ferment. Both avenues are indispensable for the alchemical journey to take its full course. Without the steadfast, patient, character-building

تو آنذ ایتاد ایاد ازسر خویش زسپ و چون پایز باشد و خارک خرما

سخ شود پای شتر مرغ ابند اکنه بسرخی وچوان خارک زنک می نماید

تا با خورسپیدن خرما و بدین سبب شتر مرغ را در عرب خاصب خوانند

یعنی پی رنک کرده و نه با مرغ البس دارد و نه باشتر و مستوحش باشد

وچون اورا در خانه بدارد بسیار زیان کند واکرکه شوار و دختری یا بامردانی

پند ربامید و بخورد و باشد که کوش شبکپله پوست خایه ا و در سرک نگند

بنه ایسته دارکیاان واکر دردیک کند با آتش انذک که بجوشد وکوبیدی آتش

ازجوش بیداآرد صفت کلنک در پریدن بانوه باشند برسقی

وکی هشیار رود و دیکری ذا مپش آ و چنین کلیک براان دیکر میکند ر تا اول

بافزاید وریاست ورسموان بهه برسه و بش پاس ازندو ازآنکه نوبت با

کبیایی برکیرد تا خواب رو غله بکند و نخسبد تا انکاه که نوبت نویس نزبپا

وچون دیکری برخیزه او برآسا بد وکلنک ه وکلاغ الا ایکا ایکا یی بخند که ازمرد

Two herons, from
Nuzhat-Namah I'Ala'i,
a sixteenth-century
picture on vellum.

progress through the *maqamat* (or valleys), the *ahwal* are nothing but fleeting, intoxicating moments with no more substance than froth upon water. Mystical states are compared to colors or to flavors. Each color, each flavor, portrays an aspect of the inner reality of the Sufi. But in the ultimate mystical experience, says Attar:

> *"The lovely forms and colors are undone*
> *And what seemed many things is only one."*

The ultimate state, then, which marks the mystical arrival at the longed-for union with the primordial beloved, is the annihilation (*fana*) of the individual self (not the individual body). Sometimes this summit of mystical fulfillment is called, simply, *nothingness*. Here, as a taste of this strange, ineffable, and paradoxical Sufi happy end, are a few more evocative verses from *The Conference of the Birds:*

> *All that I ever lost or ever found*
> *Is in the depths of that black deluge drowned.*
> *I too am lost; I leave no trace, no mark;*
> *I am a shadow cast upon the dark,*
> *A drop sunk in the sea, and it is vain*
> *To search the sea for that one drop again.*
> *This Nothingness is not for everyone,*
> *Yet many seek it out as I have done;*
> *And who would reach this far and not aspire*
> *To Nothingness, the pilgrim's last desire?*

8: heavenly bliss and earthly delight Lesley Smith

Happiness in the Christian Middle Ages

I was taught by God's grace to hold the faith and believe quite seriously that everything would turn out all right Lady Julian of Norwich

O *felix culpa*—Oh happy fault! Looking for happiness in the Middle Ages immediately forces us to confront one of the paradoxes at the heart of the Christian faith—that the birth of Christ and the gift of grace came about only because of the disobedience of Adam and Eve, which led to their expulsion from paradise.

Happiness from the fall

What seems at first to be disaster is turned to glory by a God who transforms "the Fall" into the Incarnation. Happiness is no longer simply the earthly delight of the paradise garden, lost to humans when they gave in to temptation. Instead, they have gained the hope of the delights of the world to come—eternal life with the vision of God. No wonder, then, that poets could exclaim, "Blessed be the time that apple taken was!"; the simple pleasures of Eden may have given way to toil and sweat in the here and now, but that was a fair exchange for everlasting joy.

This theological interpretation of happiness summarizes, no doubt, a common image of the Middle Ages: a faithful or credulous population living in miserable conditions, either truly believing or else brainwashed and terrorized by the Christian Church into obedience to established rules of morality and behavior for the sake of an unseen reward in heaven. Grimly guilt-ridden, medieval people made their way through the gloom of the present towards the glory of a future with God. Not much fun today, and only the promise of a happier tomorrow.

Of course, for some medieval people that may be a fairly accurate reflection of their lives; but it is not the whole story. And it is even arguable that more medieval people lived happier lives than we do now.

Food as pleasure

Manuscript illustration, especially in the margins of medieval texts, offers us a lot of pictures of people showing off and having fun. Scenes of banquets are perfect subjects for the bottom of a page, since the space is just right for drawing long tables spread with a tempting variety of food and drink. Eating was a surefire way to pleasure: one early English recipe book is called *Pleyn delit*. Instructions from medieval cookbooks are striking for the length of meals they seem to suggest, with numerous courses containing a vast array of ingredients. Gluttony, though, had to be avoided. As one of the seven deadly sins, *gula* was capable of leading you to eternal punishment, and in this as in many things, both theological and medical authorities counseled moderation.

Drink must be counted among the bringers of medieval pleasure. Water was often unsafe, so most medieval beverages had alcoholic

A medieval drinking session. From the late fourteenth-century manuscript, *Tractatum de Septem Vitiis*. It illustrates drunkenness as one of the Seven Vices.

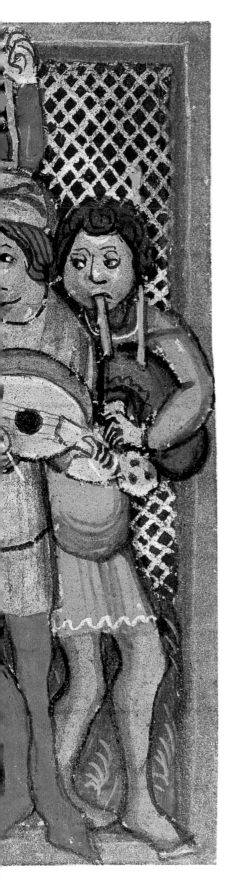

content; and although being as "drunk as a lord" was apt in numerous cases, the hard labor put in by the lower classes was relieved by some hard drinking. As so often, Geoffrey Chaucer manages to sketch in a few lines a character recognizable to most as taking it all a bit too far, in this extract from "The Franklin's Tale" from his epic *The Canterbury Tales*:

> *"His breed, his ale, was alwey after oon;*
> *A bettre envyned man was nowher noon.*
> *Without bake mete was never his hous,*
> *Of fissh and flessh, and that so plenteous*
> *It snewed in ihs hous of mete and drynke.*
> *Of alle deyntees that men koude thynke."*

Medieval comics

Chaucer reminds us just how much the people loved to laugh. Their humor runs the gamut from the sophisticated to the bawdy. Chaucer himself can be a subtle wordsmith, teasing out witty double-meanings and clever quips, then shifting to scurrilous innuendo and groaning puns. They loved it all: farce, slapstick, satire, riddles, and cruel practical jokes.

Irish monks make intricate Latin double-meanings to malign visiting Roman clergy, and they do it in plain view in ecclesiastical texts: only those clever enough to work it out could see the gag—or be offended. And most of all, medieval people loved stories: secular books are full of heroes and romance, travel and excitement. If you couldn't read, no matter: nothing was better than sitting entranced while someone else did the work, sharing the story together. Like Charles Dickens, Geoffrey Chaucer gave readings from his works to appreciative listeners.

Medieval music: a manuscript depicts medieval musicians serenading a nobleman or king. They play lute, bagpipes, triangle, horn, viola, and drum.

Medieval carnal pleasures

With sometimes surprising explicitness, medieval manuscript images depict that other great carnal pleasure, sex. From the supine to the ridiculous, no partner (not always human), no place, and no position escaped the medieval imagination. Increasingly, the Church attempted to curb these wild delights, with handbooks of penitence requiring confessors to permit sex only within marriage, at a limited number of places and times, and certainly using only a single position. It seems unlikely that they succeeded. Evidence from such "folk" sources as the Inquisition records of Montaillou—a small heretical village in Languedoc, where married women met the local priest in a nearby cellar—bolsters the impression gained from our tiny marginal scenes. Even the twelfth-century abbess and theologian, Heloise, remembered her stolen romance with Peter Abelard with defiant enjoyment: "So delectable were the lovers' joys which we sought together, that they still cannot seem displeasing to me, nor can I yet forget them."

Playing the game

Pleasure also came in the form of games. We have pictures of a huge assortment of pastimes, from bat and ball types to archery and board games such as draughts and chess. A very popular book used an allegorical version of chess as a metaphor for the fight of good against evil. Gambling was common. Hunting and hawking gave enjoyment to the rich. An emperor could write a book on hunting with birds, and hunting for deer, boar, hares, and other game was universally popular. John of Salisbury, a twelfth-century royal official, writes in his *Statesman's Book,* that things have gone too far: "hunters smack of the Centaur's training. Rarely is one found to be modest or dignified, rarely self-controlled, and in my opinion never temperate."

The margins portray other forms of entertainment: juggling, mimes, actors, singers, dancers, and players of all sorts of instrument. Music had a long and distinguished history as part of civilized society, and the academic study of music was one of the seven liberal arts. The harmony of music reflected the harmony of the spheres and of the soul, and it was for this reason that early Christian theologians recommended it as an improving occupation that could lead to greater goodness. In contrast, the lasting happiness this was meant to bring was not the same as the frivolous pleasure of love songs, bagpiping and, in John of Salisbury's words again, "the effeminate dalliance of wanton tones."

The pleasures of the hunt. A fourteenth-century prince with his falcons and his attendants.

Love

Frivolous or not, love songs lead us to love; and it is surely human love that most people today would cite as the source of their greatest happiness. As a concept, love was good, since it was a pale shadow of the love of God. But, since the Fall, it was not clear that humans could translate that love into their own terms.

Marriage was often a dynastic or material contract, and in secular literature romance seems to be evident only in the fictional and ironic constructs of "courtly love" tradition, well outside the realms of marriage and family. In the theory of the time, women were the weaker and irrational sex, to be avoided if possible and kept under strict control if not; nevertheless we can get some sense that what theory made difficult, practice made more simple, and the joys of marriage and family could be as real in the Middle Ages as they are now.

Christine de Pisan, a fourteenth-century woman who supported herself by writing and publishing after she had been widowed, wrote a memorable, ironic work, *The City of Ladies*, on how badly women were treated in the male-dominated society. And yet, she remembered her own husband with wistful joy: the longer they were married, the greater their love grew, until they became closer than brother and sister through good times and bad. He never lied to her and he encouraged her in all she did. And the feeling was not only one way: when his wife died, Count Baldwin of Guînes broke down with grief, so much so that his doctors thought they might be unable to keep him alive.

Children in medieval life

Medieval families were wider and looser than the modern Western version. Still, children were a gift from God, and love for them comes through in many places, even though infant mortality was shockingly high. St. Antony of Padua so delighted in children as the image of the baby Jesus that he is still usually depicted with a child in his arms. Philippe of Navarre, the French prince, believed that parents would not exchange their happiness in children for anything. In the early thirteenth century, Francis of Assisi made a Christmas crib at the Church at Greccio, and the Holy Family became a model for loving bonds on earth. And, of course, the archetypal image of the medieval Church was that of a mother and her newborn son.

Saint Bernard of Clairvaux taught that there is joy in abstinence.

amt bernard chapelam de la
vierge marie defcendp de la mai
son des roix de bourgongne &

Less is more: the paradox of Christian happiness

So far, we have looked at sources of medieval happiness which could be easily duplicated today; but the dominance of Christianity in the West supported another set of ideas about how happiness could be achieved. For although orthodox Christianity believed that creation was fundamentally good, there was another strand which held that all material things could only detract from the search for, and the attainment of, the spiritual life. In this view, the way to true happiness was renunciation and simplicity.

The most common method of following this path was through one of the monastic orders, chiefly the Benedictine, Cistercian, and Carthusian. In contrast to conventional wisdom that happiness was found in wealth and power, the monastic life for both sexes was lived in community, and was dedicated to ideals of poverty, chastity, and obedience to God. Founded in 1098, the Cistercians were immensely successful in attracting men and women to a life of austerity. They built their monasteries in remote rural sites, far away from the rest of the world. They lived by their own work and became renowned for their talents as farmers.

In contrast to contemporary developments in Benedictine houses, Cistercian churches had a spare, empty beauty and their liturgy rejected the ornament that had accrued elsewhere. Over time, this ideal of self-denial gave way to a more comfortable life, but the starkness of the original was hugely popular. By the end of the thirteenth century there were 740 Cistercian houses spread throughout Europe, many with hundreds of members. The most famous medieval Cistercian, Bernard of Clairvaux (1090–1153), was influential far beyond the monastery walls, advising popes and princes. He held to the most exacting interpretation of the life of abstinence, while still teaching that formal charity without an underlying feeling was not the way to joy: "Our natural inclinations entice but degrade; love that is governed by reason is arid but enduring; while love seasoned with wisdom brims over with delights."

Love seasoned with wisdom brims over with delights Bernard of Clairvaux

Joy through denial

In the first quarter of the thirteenth century, St. Francis of Assisi (1181–1226) and Dominic Guzman took the Cistercian ideal of rural self-sufficiency to the urban stage. The Dominicans and, particularly, the Franciscans lived lives where they owned nothing, relying for sustenance (sometimes to the point where they starved to death) on manual work or begging. In the space of twenty years, the ideals of the Poor Man of Assisi took the world by storm. And yet his advice on how to achieve happiness could scarcely be harder.

One bitterly cold winter's day, St. Francis was walking with Brother Leo back to Assisi from Perugia, and Leo asked Francis to tell him where perfect joy was to be found. Francis replied: when we arrive at our convent, soaked by the rain and frozen by the cold, filthy with mud and hungry, we ring the doorbell and the porter comes and angrily asks, "Who are you?" we say, "We are two of your brothers." And he contradicts us: "You are not telling the truth. You are two rascals who go around tricking people and stealing what they give to the poor. Go away!" And, with the door still closed, he makes us stand outside in the snow and rain, cold and hungry, until night falls. Then, if we endure it all patiently, the insults and rebuffs, without being upset and without complaining, and if we reflect, humbly and lovingly, that he really does know us and that it is God who makes him say these things to us, then, Brother Leo, this is perfect joy.

And if we knock again, and he curses us again, and if we bear it patiently, and take the insults with joy and love in our hearts, then, Brother Leo, this is perfect joy.

And later, suffering badly from cold and hunger, standing in the dark, we knock and call again, begging him, for God's love, to take us in; if then he comes out and attacks us with a club and beats us into the snow, and if we endure it all with joy and patience, reflecting that we must endure the sufferings of Christ patiently for love of Him, then, Brother Leo, this is perfect joy!

For, Brother Leo, above all the graces and gifts of the Holy Spirit which Christ gives to His friends is that of conquering oneself and willingly enduring suffering, insults, humiliations, and hardships for the love of Christ. For we cannot glory in all of those other marvelous gifts of God, for they are not ours but God's; but we can glory in the cross of tribulations and afflictions, because that is ours!

We can glory in the cross of tribulations and afflictions, because that is ours! St. Francis of Assisi

This story, from the fourteenth-century collection called the *Little Flowers of St. Francis*, illustrates that side of medieval happiness forged from an ascetical theology of suffering. Francis was by no means a gloomy man: he liked to sing in French; he sometimes played an imaginary violin; he loved nature and animals; he was fond of broad theatrical effects; and yet his companions remembered him as having received (for the first time in history) the stigmata—the marks of Christ's passion on his own body. The signs of Christ's suffering were etched on Francis because Francis wished to suffer along with Him, and so reach perfect joy.

Inward radiance

Francis was undoubtedly an extremist, and even Brother Leo may have found the story went rather too far for comfort. Certainly, most of the citizens of Assisi, while deeply admiring their local saint, were not too keen to emulate him. But from a Christian standpoint, Francis reflects a long tradition of bodily denial as preparation for spiritual growth. The body and all its appetites can never be a source of true pleasure, so they must be denied and suppressed to make room for something more real. Done wholeheartedly, this makes the practitioner shine with an inward radiance, in spite of outward conditions of squalor or pain. Francis is written about as a cheerful man, joyful and delighted with life, but his way to happiness was the imitation of the way of the Cross.

Giotto di Bondone (c.1266–1337)
The Ecstasy of St. Francis

The gift of many tears

Contemplating the crucifixion of Jesus of Nazareth led Francis to his own stigmata. It led other medieval mystics, particularly women, to an affective sympathy with the bodily suffering of Jesus and an overwhelming remorse for human disobedience and sinfulness. In the thirteenth, fourteenth, and fifteenth centuries, this commonly expressed itself in unstoppable bouts of tears.

Clare of Assisi, Francis' spiritual friend, was said to have had "the gift of many tears, having great compassion for the sisters and the afflicted. She especially poured out many tears when she received the body of our Lord Jesus Christ." Mary of Oignies was said to cry unceasingly, as was Clare's near contemporary, Angela of Foligno. Margery Kempe, fifteenth-century English laywoman and autobiographer extraordinary, describes her uncontrollable tears at the sin of the world. Some of those who knew Margery found this behavior difficult to bear; worse, they suspected it of being self-serving. Margery herself seems to have been uncertain. She sought the advice of her saintly but level-headed neighbor, the anchoress Julian of Norwich, who told her: "When God visits a creature with tears of contrition, devotion, or compassion, he may and ought to believe that the Holy Ghost is in his soul."

Signs of happiness then and now

Plainly, for a Christian, the imprimatur of the Holy Spirit must be a cause—indeed, the chief cause—of happiness. Yet continual crying is a long way from cosmetics, fine clothes, and successful ambitions as a sign of medieval happiness. How, then, can we recognize happiness when we see it?

Some gestures are universal; others are more difficult to read. Just as it sought to restrain what it saw as excessive physical desires, so the medieval Christian Church sought to restrain their outward expression. Readers of Umberto Eco's *Name of the Rose* will remember the plot turning on the destruction of a copy of Aristotle's lost work on laughter. The disapproval or suspicion of laughter is an old monastic standard, going back at least to the sixth-century Rule of St. Benedict: "Guard your lips from harmful or deceptive chatter, nothing just to provoke laughter; do not love immoderate or boisterous laughter." Bernard of Clairvaux agreed: "It is disgraceful for others to incite you to derisive laughter; it is more disgraceful for you to elicit such laughter from them."

The Poor Clares at service, from the psalter
of Richard II (1367–1400) of England.

The Gothic smile

The point of medieval life was not to seem gloomy. Francis told off a friar who looked cheerless: "Before me and the rest strive ever to be joyful; for it is not right for the servant of God to show sadness and a dismal face." The value placed on crying for Christ and the strictures against laughter are warnings against immoderation, denigration, and spitefulness, and one could tell laughter was wrong because of the disorder that it elicited from the face and the body. The height of happiness is shown instead by order in the limbs, a calm countenance, and what has been termed "the Gothic smile." We can see Gothic smiles on angels and humans among the sculptures of European medieval cathedrals, such as Bamberg and Reims (above). The saved, on the right hand of Christ, smile a closed-mouth, Cheshire-cat grin, which can strike the modern viewer as a little sinister. We have difficulty interpreting this as the apogee of joy: not enough is happening; the wearers seem too composed; they look smug and complacent.

A gothic smile from an angel. The Annunciation on the west portal of Reims cathedral (built in the twelfth century), in France.

The damned, on the other hand, are full of movement; their smiles show bare teeth, their limbs gyrate, and their bodies are set at awkward angles. They look like a crowd of disco dancers—a little drunk, perhaps, but just out for a good time. But the disorder of their bodies signals to the medieval viewer that they are out of harmony with God. They have lost their place in the order of the universe, and it is upon this order that all happiness, in the Christian view, depends.

> *"In the beginning God created the heavens and the earth... and God saw everything that he had made, and, behold, it was very good."* (Genesis 1)

The book of Genesis told medieval people how their world had come about. It was a deliberate, ordered creation springing from the mind of a single, good being: God. Since humans had been created by God, they could find no better happiness than in conforming to God's will and, eventually, in life in the presence of the Divine. The book of Revelation told them what would happen at the end of the world. After a series of hideous signs and portents, angels with trumpets would open the book of the saved and the damned, sending each person to his or her allotted place, either in sight of God or far from God's presence, tormented by the loss of the good.

Vision of God

Two of the principal metaphors used by Revelation to describe the life of heaven tell us something of how the early Christians saw happiness. The Church meets Christ adorned as a bride for her husband; and at that spiritual union, the guests—the saved—sit down at a wedding banquet. Food, family, and sex come once again to the fore as sources of human joy, even in this new heavenly context. Medieval theologians could not gainsay the authority of the Bible, but they also stressed the rather more decorous happiness of the saved in seeing God: the Beatific Vision.

The desire to see the Creator has long biblical roots, going back all the way to Moses. Paul's letter to the Corinthians promised that, though we now see only dimly, as if in a mirror, in heaven we shall see God face to face—a privilege granted, we know from Jesus' Sermon on the Mount, to the pure in heart. According to the first letter of John, the purpose of seeing God "just as he is," is to change, for then "we shall be like him." The vision of God makes humans sinless, acting in perfect charity, and it must last forever, since nothing less than eternal beatitude would be perfect beatitude. It—and only it—brings perfect happiness; it is the ultimate end.

Who will go to heaven?

Scholastic theologians worked hard to complicate this fairly simple idea, asking who might attain it, when, and how. They found the arguments difficult, even among themselves, raising issues such as what sort of understanding was required to contemplate the divine being. Yet essentially, the concept is easy to grasp, and all medieval people would be able to know that the final and greatest happiness was life with God.

Of course, it was not quite so straightforward to know who might get there, but Christian theology was clear that worldly status was not a factor: God might order "the rich man in his castle, the poor man at his gate" on this earth, but the queue for heaven had different rules and everyone had the chance of a place. In the *Divine Comedy* (completed by 1321), Dante put popes in hell and beggars in heaven.

Not all medieval people can have believed in God, or in the biblical view of heaven. Nevertheless, we can be reasonably confident that more medieval people believed than people do today. Perhaps this sense of a fundamental order, of purpose, of a guiding hand, gave them a greater sense of security, which we might interpret as happiness.

A lot of modern energy is expended in a search for "meaning," which would not have been so when the Christian explanation of the world was still dominant. It did not stop many people from trying as hard as they could to have a good time in the here and now, although it is true that the numbers who were attracted to the self-effacement of religious orders were considerable. Nevertheless, the Middle Ages were still a time when God was likely to be in his heaven and, in the words of Julian of Norwich, "I was taught by God's grace to hold steadfastly to the faith I had already learned, and at the same time to believe quite seriously that everything *would* turn out all right."

Before me and the rest strive ever to be joyful; for it is not right for the servant of God to show sadness and a dismal face St. Francis of Assisi

Lady Julian of Norwich (1343–1443) lived in religious isolation, writing her *XVI Revelations of Divine Love*. They were not published until 1760.

9: in praise of reason Jill Kraye

From humanism to Descartes

*Happy is he who goods of body
and soul attains
And also the gifts of the goddess
Fortune gains* Filippo Beroaldo

The Renaissance is known as a period of cultural rebirth and renewal. One of the many factors that contributed to this reawakening was the rise of humanism, a scholarly program aimed at recovering, restoring, and reviving the legacy of classical antiquity. Humanists were involved not only in the recovery of the written and physical remains of ancient Greece and Rome; they also engaged in the interpretation, assimilation, and imitation of the ideas and values that these literary and material artifacts embodied and represented.

For all their devotion to antiquity, however, humanists were men of their own times, living in a culture dominated by Christianity. They had to find ways of combining the classical ideas of happiness with the Christian concept of happiness, both of which meant different things to them.

Petrarch—father of humanism

The Italian poet and scholar Francesco Petrarca (1304–74), known to the English-speaking world as Petrarch, is generally regarded as the father of the humanist movement. Most of the topics discussed by later humanists were first broached by him, and the theme of happiness is no exception. His treatment of this subject involved a subtle blending of Christian teaching and classical philosophy, drawing, in particular, on doctrines associated with Roman Stoicism. Petrarch's *Remedies for Fortune Fair and Foul* consists of a series of dialogues, in which the main speaker is Reason, which the Stoics regarded as the best—indeed, only—guide to human behavior. Reason lectures various characters representing Sorrow, Fear, Joy, and Hope, which the Stoics regarded as pathological emotional states that had to be thoroughly rooted out, because of the need to avoid depression in the face of adversity and elation in the face of prosperity.

Falling into the second category is a dialogue on Happiness, in which Joy repeatedly claims to be happy. Reason attempts to demonstrate that these feelings of happiness are short-lived and illusory. "Perhaps you think the papacy, empire, or power and wealth in general make one happy," says Reason—yet "if they do anything, they bring misery rather than happiness." Parading his classical learning, Petrarch has Reason go on to show that great figures from antiquity, such as Alexander the Great and Julius Caesar, were never happy since "their lives were continuously disturbed and turbulent."

Although no explicitly Christian arguments are brought into the dialogue, the lesson taught by Reason turns out to be in complete accord with the dictates of faith: "no one is happy until he moves out of this vale

Petrarch (Francesco Petrarca) was crowned poet laureate of Rome in a public ceremony in April 1340.

of miseries." The Stoic notion that one should respond to brief spells of good fortune with rational detachment rather than emotional rejoicing is here unobtrusively merged with the Christian belief that true happiness can be achieved only in the next life.

The themes aired by Petrarch were taken up and developed by many Italian humanists of the fifteenth century. The Neapolitan scholar Bartolomeo Facio (c.1405–57), for instance, wrote a Latin dialogue entitled *The Happiness of Man*, in which he dwelt on the innumerable trials and tribulations of the present life, especially those suffered by men of letters unable to find patrons willing to support them—a subject dear to the heart of all humanists. The happiness sought by man, according to Facio, was not to be found in any pursuit or achievement in worldly terms: not in wealth, power, dignity, glory, kingship, military exploits, the priesthood, or even literary studies. It was consequently necessary not only to use reason to keep our desires and emotions in check, but also to cultivate the Christian virtues of faith, hope, and charity, that would ultimately enable us to find happiness in the next life.

Perhaps you think the papacy, empire, or power and wealth make one happy, yet if they do anything, they bring misery rather than happiness Petrarch

Humanist happiness and unhappiness

As Christians concerned with the fate of their immortal souls, all humanists shared the conviction of Petrarch and Facio that real happiness could be attained only in the afterlife. Some nevertheless took a more positive view of the possibilities of procuring a limited degree of happiness during man's brief time on earth.

These humanists celebrated the gifts that had been given to man to make use of and enjoy in the present life: a body that surpassed all other created beings in beauty and symmetry because it had been made in God's image and likeness; and a mind so powerful that it was capable of such marvelous feats as the construction of the cupola of the Florentine cathedral and the invention of printing. The most famous humanist hymn to humanity was the *Oration on the Dignity of Man* by the princely philosopher Giovanni Pico della Mirandola (1463–92).

Everything everywhere is tinged with bitterness Desiderius Erasmus

Unlike the rest of creation, man had been granted by God the freedom to fashion himself into whatever form of life he chose. This meant that he could sink to the level of a brute animal or lead a merely vegetative existence; but it also allowed him to rise to the heights of an almost divine being by giving himself over entirely to the life of the mind through the study of philosophy.

The other side of such humanist exaltations of man's potential to achieve a degree of happiness while on earth were humanist laments over the inescapable unhappiness of our mortal existence, unrelieved by considerations of future bliss in the next life. Among the more depressing representatives of this dismal genre is the dialogue *On the Misery of the Human Condition* by the Florentine scholar and papal bureaucrat, Poggio Bracciolini (1380–1459). His lifelong obsession with the idea of the instability of human affairs, ruled over by capricious fortune, was confirmed by the fall of Constantinople to the Turks in 1453, a traumatic event for European Christendom and the inspiration for this deeply pessimistic work.

Not only did fortune's arbitrary power overturn cities, empires, and kingdoms, its recklessness and random violence afflicted every aspect of human life, which was "consumed by wretchedness." Nor could we protect ourselves by using our reason, since it had been fatally weakened and depraved by original sin, making it vulnerable to the constant assaults of human stupidity and vice.

These gloomy themes had a surprisingly wide resonance and long shelf-life in the supposedly optimistic era of the Renaissance. By the early sixteenth century, however, such ideas had become sufficiently hackneyed to be made fun of by the Dutch humanist Desiderius Erasmus (c.1469–1536). He has the allegorical figure of Folly, the mock heroine of his satirical masterpiece, *The Praise of Folly*, comically bemoan the fact that "man is besieged by a whole army of diseases, threatened by accidents, assailed by misfortunes," so that "everything everywhere is tinged with bitterness."

Next page: A renaissance flowering: Raphael's (1483–1520) impression of classical philosophers, *The School of Athens*, Plato and Aristotle center.

Stoic happiness

Stoicism was the philosophy of choice for Renaissance thinkers such as Poggio who were inclined to focus on the insecurity and unhappiness of man's earthly life. For, according to Stoic precepts, the truly wise man—an endangered species in antiquity as in the Renaissance—would be happy even if his physical condition and material circumstances were wretched, as long as the virtuous state of his soul remained intact. As we have seen in relation to Petrarch's *Remedies*, this state of virtue and happiness was achieved by living in accordance with reason and refusing to yield to the irrational impulses of the emotions.

Another Italian humanist who was attracted to the Stoic view of happiness was Angelo Poliziano (1454–94), the most learned classical scholar of the fifteenth century. In 1479, he translated from Greek into Latin the *Handbook* of the ex-slave turned Stoic philosopher, Epictetus. In his dedication (to his patron, Lorenzo de Medici, 1449–92, the unofficial ruler of Florence), Poliziano stressed that Epictetus's philosophy, which sought to make men invulnerable to fear, pain, and other emotional disturbances, was a particularly appropriate text for the troubled times in which they were living. It alluded to a recent conspiracy that had threatened Lorenzo's life and his regime.

Periods of political and social turmoil tended to make the rather grim and austere Stoic notion of happiness more appealing. The last quarter of the sixteenth century, when much of northern Europe was torn apart by civil and religious wars, thus proved to be an opportune moment for a large-scale revival of Stoic philosophy. Its teachings were attractively packaged by the Flemish humanist Justus Lipsius (1547–1606), who stressed their compatibility with Christianity and presented the cardinal Stoic virtue of steadfastness as the best means to gain peace of mind—the rational happiness allowed by Stoicism—in the middle of public calamity.

The vogue for Stoicism, set in motion by Lipsius, spread throughout Europe, and lasted well into the seventeenth century. Its ideal of happiness was popularized in many languages, including English. In the essay, "He is an happy man," published in 1608, Bishop Joseph Hall (1574–1656) describes the character of the happy man, saying he "knowes the world, and cares not for it." He can therefore take disasters in his stride: "if his ship be tossed, yet he is sure his Anchor is fast." Hall, like Petrarch three centuries earlier, places this classical image within a Christian framework: the happy man's "eyes stick so fast in heaven, that no earthly object can remove them."

This detail from Cosimo Rosselli's (1439–1507) *Procession of the Bishop in front of the Church of S. Ambrogio* shows the scholar Poliziano, the celebrated philosopher Mirandola, and the philosopher Ficino.

Aristotelian happiness

The Greek philosopher Aristotle held a very different view of happiness from the Stoics; and since his writings virtually monopolized university teaching from the thirteenth to the seventeenth centuries, this notion was inculcated into generation upon generation of scholars. According to Aristotle, happiness consisted of a life-long activity in accordance with the highest virtue, which in his opinion was philosophical contemplation—as a philosopher himself, he naturally awarded the highest rank to his own favorite pursuit. While the Stoics insisted that all one needed for happiness was a virtuous soul, Aristotle believed that in order to contemplate, and thus be happy, it was necessary to have at least a minimum of physical well-being and material comfort: an empty stomach would eventually call a halt to even the most profound philosophizing. The Aristotelian formula for happiness was summed up by a Renaissance humanist in a handy Latin couplet,

> *Happy is he who goods of body and soul attains*
> *And also the gifts of the goddess Fortune gains.*

Wand of Mercury, Horn of Plenty

Aristotle's concept of happiness was very widely diffused in Renaissance culture, often appearing in watered-down versions that made no reference to Aristotle. A typical instance can be observed in the *Iconologia*, a manual for deciphering the meaning of allegorical images by the Italian art theorist Cesare Ripa (c.1555–1622). He describes the figure of "Happiness" as a women holding a caduceus, the wand of the god Mercury, in her right hand and a cornucopia, or horn of plenty, in her left. This image, which was illustrated by a woodcut in later editions of the *Iconologia*, was well known to humanists from their study of Roman coins, and it appeared in various paintings of the period, such as *The Allegory of Happiness* by the Florentine artist Agnolo Bronzino (1503–72). Explaining the two attributes held by "Happiness," Ripa, without mentioning Aristotle, says that the caduceus signifies virtue and the cornucopia of riches: "for those among us who are happy have sufficient earthly goods to provide for the needs of the body and sufficient virtue to relieve the needs of the soul."

Angelo Bronzino (1503–72) *The Allegory of Happiness*. Happiness holds the wand of Mercury in her right hand and the horn of plenty in her left.

Aristotle's view of happiness, like all such classical notions, had to be made compatible with Christianity. The process here was rather different from that applied to Stoicism. It was argued that although complete and perfect happiness could not be obtained until the next life, there was nonetheless an incomplete and imperfect happiness that could be achieved here on earth. It had been discussed by Aristotle. The two forms of happiness were certainly different, but they were not in conflict. This compromise solution allowed humanists, philosophers, and even theologians to endorse the Aristotelian concept of earthly happiness without undermining their religious belief in the Christian happiness of the future life. The devout Flemish monk, Dionysius the Carthusian (1402/3–71), could thus maintain that even though in our present existence we can see God only through a glass darkly, it is still possible for us to achieve the limited happiness described by Aristotle, which is both a foretaste of, and the first step towards, the absolute happiness that will be our reward in the future life.

The horn of plenty, here held by a Renaissance Mediterranean trader, symbolized riches. For Aristotelians they were an underpinning of happiness, although not a part of happiness.

Platonic happiness

Adjustments and compromises were not necessary in relation to the Platonic notion of happiness: the contemplation and enjoyment of God by the immortal soul after it has been released at death from its imprisonment in the body. The closeness of this concept to the Christian view of happiness was an important factor in the Renaissance revival of Plato—his pagan belief in the preexistence and transmigration of souls, on the other hand, tended to be swept under the carpet. The harmony between Platonism and Christianity was of particular importance to the key figure in that revival, the Florentine philosopher and theologian, Marsilio Ficino (1433–99), who combined a career in the priesthood with his scholarly activities as a translator and interpreter of Plato. In a letter "On Happiness," written in 1473 to his student, the young Lorenzo de Medici, Ficino presented a seamless combination of Platonic and Christian themes, leading to the conclusion that "true happiness is the property of the soul which, when freed from the body, contemplates the divine" and experiences the joy of loving God. Lorenzo then transformed his teacher's learned Latin epistle into an Italian lyric poem, in which he describes the state of the soul in the present life, "bound in carnal bonds, confined within this prison's gloom," and the liberation of "the happy soul" as it achieves its ultimate consummation by contemplating and loving God.

Just as the affinity of Platonism to Christianity fueled its revival in fifteenth-century Italy, so too it played a crucial role in the late flowering of interest in Platonism that occurred in seventeenth-century Britain. The moving force behind this resurgence was a group of learned divines known as the Cambridge Platonists, who, like Ficino, were committed to both Platonic philosophy and Christian theology. One of their number, the Regius Professor of Hebrew, Ralph Cudworth (1617–88), drew heavily on Platonism in his battle against the atheistic tendencies he feared were being fostered by the scientific revolution then under way. In his *True Intellectual System of the Universe*, aimed at demonstrating that Christian beliefs had the support of reason as well as revelation, he showed that not only the Bible but also Platonic philosophy held that "our human souls" would attain true happiness only when they were freed from "the prisons, or living sepulchres" of our "gross" bodies.

True happiness is the property of the soul which, when freed from the body, contemplates the divine Marsilio Ficino

Epicurean happiness

Epicurus's firm rejection of the immortality of the soul and of divine providence made his ethical beliefs, including his equation of happiness with pleasure, too hot for most Renaissance thinkers to handle. In the mid-seventeenth century, however, the French priest, humanist, and philosopher, Pierre Gassendi (1592–1655), made Epicureanism safe for Christians by drastically modifying some of its basic premises.

Epicurean happiness could then come into its own. It was, in fact, quite tame: for him it was a state of tranquillity, free from physical pain and mental anxiety, that brings the greatest pleasure we are able to experience. Gassendi and others showed that Epicurus's school in Athens, known as "The Garden," was not an iniquitous den of self-indulgence, but rather a haven of temperate, sober, and virtuous well-being.

This rehabilitated Epicurean conception of happiness gained many adherents in the second half of the seventeenth century, not least the English scholar and diplomat Sir William Temple (1628–99). His *Upon the Garden of Epicurus*, an idyllic account of Epicurean happiness, concluded with a leisurely disquisition on the wholesome pleasures of "Gardening in the year 1685."

Cartesian happiness

Having begun with the father of humanism, Petrarch, it is appropriate to conclude with the father of modern philosophy, René Descartes (1596–1650), the French thinker who initiated a decisive turn away from the ancient notions of happiness revived and Christianized during the Renaissance. In the 1640s Descartes retained enough respect for classical philosophy, specifically Stoicism, to select Seneca's *On the Happy Life* for discussion in his correspondence with Princess Elizabeth of the Palatinate (1618–80). He soon discovered, however, that the Roman philosopher's views on happiness were "not sufficiently accurate to deserve to be followed"; for Seneca failed to "see clearly what makes a life happy."

In Descartes's opinion, "to live happily" was "to have a perfectly content and satisfied mind." To secure this inner contentment, one required "a firm and constant resolution to carry out whatever reason recommends without being diverted by passion." This formula for rational happiness appears to differ little from that of the Stoics. But Descartes departed radically from all ancient schools of philosophy in the means for regulating the passions: they were to be systematically reprogrammed through scientific knowledge of our psycho-physiological responses. Descartes's belief that it was science, not ancient philosophy or Christianity, that held the key to human happiness marks the beginning of a brave, new modern world.

Evoking the Epicurean idea of happiness is *The Artist and his Family in Concert* by David Teniers (1610-90).

10: the greatest happiness of the greatest number Geoffrey Scarre

Utilitarianism and Enlightenment

Nature has placed mankind under two sovereign masters, pain *and* pleasure Jeremy Bentham

In 1768, a young Englishman, uncertain of his course in life, chanced to pick up a recently published pamphlet in the library of an Oxford coffee house. The pamphlet—Joseph Priestley's *Essay on Government*—and especially a particular expression in it jolted and delighted him; he cried out as it were in an inward ecstasy like Archimedes on the discovery of the fundamental principle of hydrostatics, "Eureka!" All his doubts vanished. His path in life lay clear before him: he would work to promote *the greatest happiness of the greatest number.*

The usefulness of happiness

The young man was the twenty-year-old Jeremy Bentham (1748–1832), Oxford graduate and newly qualified barrister. His father, a prosperous London attorney, had raised his son to follow in the paternal footsteps and take up the comfortable, lucrative career of a lawyer. But Jeremy's coat was cut from a very different cloth. The more he learned of the law of England, the more appaled he became by its obscurantism, its haphazard inconsistency, the complacency and conservatism of its practitioners, and its frequent serious failure to deliver justice. Instead of becoming a lawyer, Bentham would become a critic of the law, an advocate of a more rational, scientific, and humane approach to legislation and the organization of the legal system.

Noted author and critic Sir Leslie Stephen (1832–1904) described Bentham as putting the question, "What is the use of you?" to every law and institution. "Was a thing useful?"—that, for Bentham, was the acid test. Whatever lacked "utility"—a term he adopted from the Scottish philosopher David Hume (1711–76)—should be disposed of as speedily as possible. By "utility," Bentham explained that he meant "property in any object, whereby it tends to produce benefit, advantage, pleasure, good, or happiness, or to prevent the happening of mischief, pain, evil, or unhappiness to the party whose interest is considered," whether an individual or society at large. This emphasis on the felt quality of experience he justified by reference to the empirically grounded premise that happiness was what human beings actually most wanted: "The consequences of any Law, or of any act which is made the object of a Law—the only consequences that men are at all interested in—what are they but *pain* and *pleasure*?"

Jeremy Bentham, who arranged in his will for his remains to be stuffed. With a wax face, they are on display in University College, London.

Blueprints for reform

Convinced that it was not enough merely to paint out the shortcomings of existing institutions, Bentham devoted the whole of his long life to composing meticulous blueprints for radical change in virtually every field of public life. He was not only reformist in spirit himself, but spurred reforming thoughts in others.

Gathering around him a coterie of like-minded men and women, variously termed *utilitarians*, *Benthamites*, and *philosophic radicals*, Bentham became in the new century the idol of progressives and the *bête noire* of traditionalists. His numerous books and articles applied the principle of utility to all manner of subjects from church and parliamentary reform to the design of schools and prisons; and, as nothing relevant to improving the quality of life was beneath his notice, they frequently display a concern for detail which can seem to border on the obsessive.

From Bentham's highly practical perspective, vague and unfleshed ideas were of no use to anyone. Like Karl Marx, he believed that the philosopher's primary task was to change the world—or at least to supply some precise instructions for changing it. He thought it no less his business to consider the merits of different kinds of filling for the prisoners' mattresses in a model jail than to ponder the constitution of an ideal republic or the conditions for universal peace.

The Enlightenment

Bentham did not invent the slogan, "the greatest happiness of the greatest number," even if his is the name that nowadays we chiefly associate with it. Its ultimate origins are still a matter for scholarly debate, though a good case has been made for attributing its earliest use to the German philosopher Leibniz, in a book review published in 1700. What is indisputable is that it became a central ethical principle of the eighteenth-century Enlightenment—sometimes stated, often implied.

The Enlightenment was a complex intellectual and social phenomenon, characterized by a new confidence in human powers to understand and control the world (assisted by developments in natural science, medicine, and economic theory), an impatience with traditional sources of authority, whether religious or political, a focus on the things of this life rather than on the soul's ultimate destiny, and an intensified concern—in many Enlightenment thinkers, a driving passion—to better the condition of the poor, the suffering, and the powerless.

The Enlightenment has been well-described as the prelude to modernity and certainly many of the features of the contemporary western world which we take for granted—such as universal education and healthcare, political rights and privileges for all, freedom of thought and expression—are the legacies, at least in part, of battles fought and won by the champions of the Enlightenment and their nineteenth-century successors.

The nature machine

"Enlightenment," according to the writings of the German philosopher Immanuel Kant (1724–1804) in 1784, "is man's emergence from his self-incurred immaturity": "self-incurred" because (Kant thought) it was from a lack of confidence in their own abilities that people preferred to trust to the guidance of authorities who really knew no more than themselves. "The motto of enlightenment is therefore: *Dare to know.* Have courage to use your *own* understanding!" That man could, by his own intelligence and effort, master the secrets of nature been triumphantly demonstrated by the seventeenth-century scientific revolution, in particular by the towering achievements of Sir Isaac Newton (1642–1727). And what that revolution had revealed was that nature, for all its surface complexities, was a regular, law-governed structure—in effect, a gigantic machine. Finding out how the machine operated offered the prospect of harnessing natural forces to human ends; man who had previously been the awestruck and impotent spectator of God's creation would be man the ingenious, manipulative engineer.

Dare to know. Have courage to use your own understanding! Immanuel Kant

The science of man

Human beings were themselves a part of the natural order; so human nature, too, must be subject to laws. If these could be identified by application of the same inductive and empirical methods that had proved so successful in uncovering the secrets of inanimate nature, the resulting knowledge would not just be of academic interest. Understanding precisely what kind of creature man was, how his mental processes worked, what motives drove him, what potential and capacities he possessed, how fixed or malleable a character he had, would help immensely in the redesigning of the social environment and its institutions. Eighteenth-century thinkers addressed themselves enthusiastically to the science of man. To many of these philosophers it seemed obvious that a fundamental—according to some, *the* fundamental—driving force of human beings was the desire for happiness. It is "happiness," asserted the Baron d'Holbach (1723–89), "toward which our own nature obliges us eternally to tend." Claude Helvétius (1715–71) thought that men had an "irresistible inclination" to seek their own individual good, which was happiness. While for Bentham: "Nature has placed mankind under two sovereign masters, *pain* and *pleasure*"—masters whose yoke, being law-bound, was inescapable. "They govern us in all we do, in all we say, in all we think: every effort we can make to throw off our subjection will serve but to demonstrate and confirm it." In his *Essay on Man*, the poet Alexander Pope (1688–1744) expressed it most succinctly: "Oh Happiness! Our being's end and aim."

If happiness is what human beings are innately disposed to seek, there will be nothing very meritorious about a person's pursuing his own happiness; he is simply doing what comes naturally. Moral praise is earned by those who work to promote the happiness of others. Voltaire (1694–1778) sounded a common Enlightenment note when he defined "*vertu*" in his *Dictionnaire Philosophique* in 1764 as "beneficence towards one's neighbor." So-called virtues that served only the subject's interests (such as the traditional "theological virtues" of faith and hope in

God, which helped one to get to heaven) were not genuine virtues, since they failed to be "useful" to other people. The others that we should help include all those who share our human nature, regardless of their gender, race, nation, class, or religious affiliation. Some of the philosophers, including Voltaire and Bentham, thought that non-human animals too, as beings capable of feeling pleasure and pain, possessed some moral standing and should be treated kindly.

"All men," wrote Thomas Jefferson (1743–1826) in that defining document of the Enlightenment, the American Declaration of Independence, "are created equal," with the same "unalienable rights" to "life, liberty, and the pursuit of happiness." While the fine principles professed by the philosophers were not always fully lived up to in practice (Jefferson himself, for instance, was a slave-owner all his life), the theory at least was clear: all human beings mattered, and mattered in the same degree.

That all people mattered equally was a tenet of utilitarianism. It was enshrined in the American Declaration of Independence, the signing of which is captured here by artist John Trumbull.

Utilitarian thinkers

Not all the statements of utilitarianism's maximizing principle are to be found in writers we would think of primarily as philosophers (though the distinction between philosophers and non-philosophers was less clear-cut in the eighteenth century than now). The great Italian jurist, Cesare Beccaria (1738–94), declared near the beginning of his influential *Trattato dei delitti e delle pene* (Treatise of Crimes and Punishments) (1764) that the proper end of society and its institutions was "the greatest happiness divided amongst the greatest number." Ten years later the French historian Jean François, Marquis de Chastellux (1734–88), in his essay *De la félicité publique*, could claim it to be "an acknowledged truth" that "the first object at all governments, should be to render the people happy." Chastellux admitted that previous ages had failed to discover how to bring about the general happiness. But that was no reason not to go on trying; it was possible to learn from the mistakes of the past, while recent advances in industry and agriculture raised hopes that the degrading poverty and drudgery of the masses could be eradicated. In time, thought Chastellux, increases in knowledge and political liberties would undoubtedly lead to "the acquisition of the greatest happiness of the greatest number."

Claude Helvétius shared his countryman's conviction that the human lot was capable of betterment. In his famous *De l'esprit* of 1758 (later described by Bentham as his "favorite book"), Helvétius argued that men could be made happy through the fulfilment of their fundamental desires for food, drink, sleep, shelter, sex, and friendship. It was unnecessary for them to strive to be wealthy, powerful, or privileged at the expense at others; indeed, rich people tended to be relatively unhappy because they lacked the satisfaction of fulfilling their basic wants by their own efforts. Human beings were at bottom self-interested, Helvétius thought, yet good laws and education could mold individuals into cooperative citizens of communities which enjoyed a high average level of happiness. (Helvétian education, however, includes attempting to wash out any antisocial desires which a person may happen to have: a somewhat disquieting program of mind-control, as many critics have noted.) "Public utility," or the utility of "the greatest number," was the ultimate test of all laws and institutions, and people became virtuous once they learned to identify their personal interests with the general.

The price of utility

Happiness, as far as it concerned the Scottish philosopher Francis Hutcheson (1694–1746), consisted of "the full enjoyment of all the gratifications its nature desires and is capable of." As early as 1725,

Knowledge in the cause of utility

Social thinking in the Enlightenment was no mere utopian dreaming; the object, vigorously and intelligently pursued, was to discover the practical means towards creating the kingdom of man on earth. The great *Encyclopédie*, edited by Denis Diderot (1713–84) and Jean d'Alembert (1717–83) between 1751 and 1776, explored in minute detail advances in the arts and sciences, commerce, technology, industry, and agriculture that promised, if the forces of conservatism could be overcome, to make the human lot a happier one. Happiness was what everyone desired; and therefore happiness, in the ethical perspective of Enlightenment writers, was what they should get. In an age which increasingly measured the worth of things in terms of their outcomes, social institutions too were subject to a productivity criterion; they were judged according to their capacity to be efficient factories of happiness. And as human beings were equally important, it was unacceptable for them to favor the interests of some people at the expense of others. Everyone's happiness was an object worth promoting; hence the aim should be to create as much happiness as possible, for the greatest number of people.

Denis Diderot created his vast encyclopedia in order to bring together the knowledge that would make increased happiness possible.

Hutcheson was stating a fully fledged utilitarian criterion: "That action is best, which procures the greatest Happiness for the greatest Numbers; and that, worst, which, in like manner, occasions Misery." Unlike some of the other thinkers we have considered, Hutcheson believed that we are not wholly self-interested creatures, but are endowed by nature with benevolent impulses. These give rise to "a Sense of Goodness and moral Beauty in Actions, distinct from Advantage"; so that "when we are ask'd the Reason of our Approbation at any Action, we perpetually alledge its Usefulness to the Publick, and not to the Actor himself." But while our moral sense prompts us to favor actions which benefit others and disfavor those which harm them, Hutcheson thought that, for specific moral dilemmas, we had to estimate the consequences of the various options open to us and go with the one likely to produce the best. This "consequentialist" method of arriving at moral decisions was to become a *leitmotif* of subsequent utilitarianism. For Hutcheson and many later theorists, it seemed obvious that if happiness is a good thing, then the more we produce of it the better.

But this idea faces a snag, as opponents of the doctrine have been keen to point out. What should we do if we are faced with a situation in which maximizing happiness for all requires us to cause harm to a few? Should we accept that the end justifies (or even obligates) the means, and perform the harmful act, no matter how strongly doing so may go against the moral grain? Hutcheson thought that "an immense Good to few, may preponderate a small Evil to many." But what if the maximizing goal can be achieved only at the price of seriously harming an individual or minority? Would it be permissible, as the radical utilitarian William Godwin (1756–1836) argued in 1793, to "put a man to death for the common good, either because he is infected with a pestilential disease, or because some oracle has declared it essential to the public safety"?

It may seem odd that a moral doctrine which tells us to create as much happiness as possible should be subject to the charge that it sometimes enjoins us to *harm* people. Part of the reason may have been that they saw the destined sacrificial victims of their own pet happiness-enhancing schemes as mainly the rich, the powerful, and the overprivileged. Reducing the advantages which they enjoyed (often acquired unfairly) for the sake of increasing net social utility seemed morally praiseworthy rather than problematic. As the utilitarian and non-conformist minister Joseph Priestley (1733–1804) put it, if divine goodness is impartial and prefers "the happiness of the *whole* to that of any *individuals*," then so too should human justice have in view "the welfare of our fellow creatures and of mankind at large." People should contribute to one another's happiness; and if this requires voluntary or even enforced sacrifice by some, then so be it. Christ himself, thought Priestley, had set an utilitarian example by giving his own life so that all men might live.

Thomas Rowlandson's illustration of a theatrical booth at a fair in the 1820s.

Greatest happiness or greatest number?

For all the fine words of Priestley and others, it is doubtful whether the moral implications of maximization were fully thought through by the early utilitarian writers. One indirect piece of evidence for this is that no one seems to have grasped, until after the turn of the nineteenth century, that the original formulations of the greatest happiness principle are actually incoherent! In an article of 1829 Bentham claims to have noted "some years" earlier that the twin goals—of maximizing happiness and maximizing the number of people made happy—are capable of coming apart. The point can be easily shown. Imagine that I have a choice of two actions, one of which will produce a small amount of happiness (call this, with artificial precision, one unit) for each of ten people, and a second that will create five units of happiness each for five people. Which action should I perform? That depends on whether I want to produce the greatest amount of happiness or please the largest number of people: I can either create twenty-five units of happiness for five people or ten units for ten, but I cannot satisfy both maximizing demands together. Bentham considered that the maximization of happiness was the more essential utilitarian goal and proposed to drop the reference to the "greatest number"; most later utilitarians have followed suit. But he also saw that, in practice, the two maxims would rarely diverge. Real life tends to exhibit a principle of diminishing marginal returns, whereby the more of some good which a person holds, the less his happiness is enhanced by each incremental addition. Any limited quantity of goods will usually produce greater utility, if distributed among a larger than among a smaller number of persons (so long as the goods are not spread so thinly that their incremental contribution to everyone's utility is close to zero).

Pleasures and pains

Bentham was a psychological hedonist who believed that a desire for pleasure and a distaste for pain were the ultimate determinants of all human behavior. The principle of utility "both recognizes this subjection and assumes it for the foundation of that system, the object of which is to rear the fabric of felicity by the hands of reason and of law." If we are to produce happiness on earth, we first need to know what exactly it is; so Bentham set out to provide an analysis of the nature and varieties of pleasures and pains. The resulting account is a curious mix of discernment and naivety. Bentham considered that there were seven "circumstances" which determined the value of a pleasure or a pain: its intensity; its duration; its certainty or uncertainty; its closeness or remoteness; its fecundity (the chance of its being followed by other sensations of the same kind); its purity (its chance of not being followed

Gin Lane by William Hogarth (1697–1764). This is how some critics of utilitarian ethics envisaged the ultimate maximization of pleasure.

by a sensation of the opposite kind); and its extent (the number of people affected by it). And being a man who believed that analysis consisted in the making of lists, he ingeniously discriminated fourteen kinds of simple pleasures and eleven of simple pains. Yet he was far less careful to provide a *definition* of "pleasure," contenting himself with the remark that for practical purposes the terms "benefit," "advantage," "pleasure," "good," and "happiness" all came to much the same thing.

Bentham's picture has also been accused of oversimplification from a different angle. Francis Hutcheson contended that some pleasures were intrinsically more valuable than others. He thought that certain pleasures—those that accompanied "the improvement of the Soul by knowledge, or the ingenious arts"—possessed "a dignity, a perfection, or beatifick quality" that was far more important than the element of mere intensity. But Bentham rejected as humbug the notion of such distinctions of worth, famously remarking that if pushpin (a popular children's game of the period) gives as much pleasure as poetry, then it is as good. (Indeed, he thought it was probably better, since poetry can have an unpleasantly disturbing effect on the soul.) While this round dismissal of the idea of qualitative differences may indicate a certain philistinism in Bentham's outlook, it was no doubt partly prompted by his recognition that if such differences among pleasures were allowed to count alongside purely quantitative ones, then the prospect of any "scientific" calculative procedure for moral decisionmaking became even more remote. How, after all, were the relative qualities of different pleasures to be determined, and who was to say which the "better" pleasures were? And how were the two dimensions of assessment meant to be related? (How should one weigh up, for instance, the comparative merits of a low-intensity pleasure of a superior kind and a high-intensity pleasure of a lower one?) Bentham may also have feared that making qualitative judgements among pleasures would lead in turn to our making qualitative judgements about the persons whose pleasures they were: a dangerously elitist and potentially anti-democratic move.

Bentham's heir

Bentham's refusal to countenance this notion—that the worth of an activity or experience might not be wholly measurable in terms of the quantity of pleasure—appeared to the greatest of his successors to be the Achilles' heel of his philosophy. John Stuart Mill (1806-73) was raised within the Benthamite circle and groomed by his father James and by Bentham himself to be the standard bearer of utilitarian values to the next generation. But Mill was scarcely out of his teens before he became deeply disillusioned by what he saw as the narrowness of his elders' views. By his early twenties he would have found little to disagree

A calculus of pleasure

Bentham thought that numerical values could be attached to the "circumstances" of pleasures and pains, enabling the relative merits of different courses of action to be determined by arithmetical calculation, but only in principle. With more realism than he is sometimes given credit for, he conceded, "It is not to be expected that this process should be strictly pursued previously to every moral judgement, or to every legislative or judicial operation." Real life was too complex and agents' knowledge too limited for decision-making to be reduced to a simple algorithm. But if a "calculus of utility" was destined to remain a pipe dream, it was worth keeping in view as an ideal model to which actual deliberations should conform as closely as possible.

He might have been even more skeptical about the prospects for a calculus had he ever questioned another of his standard assumptions, namely that "pleasure" and "pain" are two distinctive kinds of sensation—a pleasure or a pain always being the same in its basic "feel," whatever its origin. Yet it is not really plausible to suppose that the pleasure of (say) passing an important examination, of listening to Mozart's clarinet quintet, and of drinking an exquisite Burgundy are really one and the same feeling, differing only in their sources. As several recent philosophers have noted, it is not even clear that pleasure and pain can be fully analyzed as sensational states. Some writers think that part of what it means to be pleasurably affected by something is to single-mindedly concentrate on the experience or activity in question, seeking to prolong or renew it, and warding off any potential distractions or interruptions. While we cannot go further into these complex issues here, the fact that they can be raised at all indicates that Bentham's account of pleasure and pain may face a lot more problems than he realized.

with in Karl Marx's denunciation of Bentham as "the insipid, pedantic, leather-tongued oracle of the commonplace bourgeois intelligence of the nineteenth century." Profoundly affected by the growing spirit of romanticism—which aimed to counter what was increasingly seen as the Enlightenment's excessive intellectualism by emphasizing the importance of feeling and imagination—Mill considered that the analytic habits so praised by Benthamism were "a perpetual worm at the root both of the passions and the virtues." By neglecting to cultivate feeling—and particularly a love of the finer things of life—Bentham's style of utilitarianism paradoxically threatened to obstruct happiness rather than promote it. Mill never went as far as the novelist Charles Dickens, who in *Hard Times* (1854) caricatured Benthamism as "Gradgrindism"—an arid, humorless, soul-destroying obsession with facts and calculated "improvements." He firmly believed that human life held possibilities whose existence Bentham had not guessed at: "Man is never recognized by him as a being capable of pursuing spiritual perfection as an end; of desiring, for its own sake, the conformity of his own character to his standard of excellence, without hope of good or evil from other sources than his own inward consciousness." For Mill, it was worth striving for excellence in character or mind even where the process was a painful one; it was "better to be Socrates dissatisfied than a fool satisfied," even if the life of the fool was superficially more pleasant.

One might well ask whether, with such views as these, Mill can really be counted as a utilitarian at all. Yet while he firmly dismissed what he called the "benevolentiary, soup kitchen school" of utilitarianism, he continued to believe that the good of humanity was the ultimate ethical goal, and to identify this good with happiness. His 1861 essay, *Utilitarianism*, begins with a fairly traditional statement of the utilitarian principle that actions are right in proportion as they promote pleasure, and wrong as they tend to produce pain. But the story straightaway takes a Hutchesonian turn: Mill tells us that it is quite compatible with this principle to account some kinds of pleasure as higher in quality than others. Pleasures of "mere sensation" have much less value than those of "the intellect, of the feelings and imagination, and of the moral sentiments." Mill was acutely aware that the indiscriminating hedonism of Bentham led to the charge that utilitarianism was a doctrine "fit only for swine"; it needed to be stressed that utilitarians were as well able as anyone to accommodate the fact that human beings had faculties "more exalted than the animal appetites." To the question of how we can know that one kind of pleasure is superior to another, Mill's rather limp answer is that we should rely on the verdict of persons sufficiently well-acquainted with both to produce an informed comparative assessment. These judges, he confidently assures us, will favor mentally demanding pleasures such as listening to string quartets or reading poetry over more purely physical ones such as sex or football.

We may wonder whether all judges would give their votes in the way Mill supposes (and note that the pool of competent judges is apparently restricted to those who will deliver what he thinks of as the "right" answers). Mill never fully explains what exactly is under assessment in these comparisons; is it the relative pleasurableness of different activities and experiences, or whether they have further value-adding property of a non-hedonistic sort? If Mill believed that there are values that are not reducible to pleasure, then his distance from his predecessors is greater than his opening statements in *Utilitarianism* let on. While it is likely that Mill never wholly resolved certain ambiguities in his own mind, it is notable that his most developed thoughts on happiness, in the fourth chapter of

These were the improving pleasures to which some of the utilitarians might have aspired in this painting of Charles Moran and family, by Adam Buck in 1812.

the essay, represent happiness as a complex end composed of a number of separate ends, or things desirable in themselves, including beauty, knowledge, virtue, and personal dignity and excellence. We pursue happiness by pursuing these constituent goals (Mill dubs them the "parts" of happiness); and, although he sometimes suggests that pursuing them is tantamount to pursuing pleasure, this claim may be little more than a sop to tradition. It may be pleasant to fulfill one's goals, but this does not necessarily imply—as Mill the subtle psychologist must have seen—that one's goal was pleasure all along. The attainment of desirable ends such as knowledge pleases us precisely because we ascribe an independent value to those ends, and enjoy seeing them fulfilled.

Utilitarian justice

Mill also has some interesting thoughts to offer on the troubling issue of utilitarian justice. If utilitarianism prescribes that we should always create as much happiness as possible, then it seems that we will sometimes have to create a lesser evil in order to bring about a greater good. Mill's response to this problem, albeit developed sketchily rather than systematically, is sensible and undogmatic. There may be circumstances, he thinks, in which the good of some people needs to be sacrificed for the greater good of others; such trade-offs are unfortunate, but they are occasionally unavoidable. For instance, to save a life it may be permissible, even obligatory, to steal or take by force the requisite food or medicine from someone who has enough to spare; the loss suffered by the "benefactor" in this case is trivial in comparison with the loss that would be suffered by the beneficiary were his need not met. By contrast, Kant believed we should never disobey the moral law, even where doing a small wrong will prevent a major evil.

At the same time, Mill considers that individuals have no more vital interest than their personal security, and that this interest needs to be protected by prudently chosen laws which limit the sacrifices that can normally be demanded from us. Without some constraints on what can be done to us in the name of the greater good, our lives will be wretchedly insecure and nothing will seem worth striving for except the gratification of the moment; as Mill shrewdly saw, a wholly unrestricted strategy for maximizing the general happiness would really defeat its own purpose. These thoughts gesture in the direction of a revision of the basic theory strongly favored by some twentieth-century utilitarians.

Rule- and Act-utilitarianism

The debate has now moved to "Rule-" and "Act-utilitarianism." Rule maintains that it is not individual acts but categories of action, or rules for action, that should be subjected to the utility test. If, for instance, the practice of keeping promises is in general utility-enhancing, then we should adopt the rule of always keeping our promises, even though in an exceptional case it may be clear that more utility would be produced by breaking one. If no one kept a promise without first calculating whether it would yield more utility to break it, the ensuing absence of trust in others' promises would lead to the speedy collapse of the practice. Yet act-utilitarians are prone to retort that utilitarianism is close to merging with Kant's views once it is maintained that moral rules may never be breached, and rule-utilitarians have sometimes been accused of indulging in "rule worship." It certainly seems out of keeping with the spirit of utilitarianism to insist that a promise to perform some minor service should be kept even if one could save a life elsewhere if one broke it. On the other hand, a world run on rule-utilitarian principles might be a good deal more comfortable and predictable than one managed by an act-utilitarian criterion, and offer better prospects for social cooperation.

The relative merits of act and rule forms of the theory are currently being debated by utilitarian philosophers; some are confident, and many hope, that negotiation between their respective proponents will eventually lead to a stable compromise which preserves the best features of each. Utilitarianism is still very much a living doctrine, capable of adapting itself to changing circumstances while remaining committed to its central, and inspiring, concern with the promotion of human welfare. One of the most enduring products of the Enlightenment, it continues to have a profound impact within ethics, politics, and social thinking; the utilitarian message underlies many of the themes of modern life. The practical impact of the doctrine over the past two centuries has been incalculable and there is no reason to expect its decline in the future. No one would claim that Bentham's "fabric of felicity" has yet been reached in our troubled world, but utilitarians have not lost faith that the human condition is capable of improvement—not by the kind of windy utopian schemes whose record in the twentieth century has been so disastrous, but by the careful, prudent application of knowledge and reason.

11: personality and happiness Michael Argyle

Who are the happy people?

Though the soule be not caused by the body; yet in the generall it followes the temperament of it Owen Felltham

The study of happiness became a flourishing branch of psychology in the second half of the twentieth century—starting in the 1960s with researchers such as Norman Bradburn at the University of Massachusetts. Psychologists had already given a lot of attention to depressed and unhappy people. Now they started to ask themselves: "If there are happy people as well, who are they?" At international conferences, they now exchange findings about what makes people happy, and just how happy they are. Academic journals with names such as *The Journal of Happiness Studies* began to appear, as well as substantial textbooks for university students. One of the first concerns of this research has been to look into the role of personality.

Is there such a thing as a happy personality?

The results of all kinds of research carried out over recent decades indicate that there is a kind of personality trait of happiness, in a class with other personality traits. We all experience good and bad events—and everyone has some positive and negative moods as a result—but people have different levels of happiness, and to a large degree this cannot be accounted for simply by what happens to them.

Measuring positive emotion

Part of what most people mean by happiness is being in a state of joy or euphoria. In 1966, Alden Wessman and David Ricks, working at Dartmouth and Columbia Universities, published research in which they had organized such emotions into a ten-point scale. Students were asked: "How elated or depressed, happy or unhappy, did you feel today?" They had to choose from ten replies, which were scored from one to ten, with feeling pretty depressed at the lower end of the scale, to feeling OK at number six, and complete elation at number ten. The average scores were 6.0 for men, and 6.14 for women.

This scale was used to find the average emotional state on just one day. Since emotions vary quite a lot over time, a more accurate picture of how happy someone is can be found by applying the scale on different days and averaging the results over a longer period. Such longer-term studies, however, do tend to find that happiness is persistent—a person who scores high on one day is more likely than a low scorer to score high on a later date.

Even ten to fifteen years after being interviewed for the first time, and regardless of good or bad fortune in the meantime, people are found to have stayed at much the same level of happiness. This seems to reflect a happy or unhappy disposition. It can be accounted for in part by the fact that some of our other, most stable, personality traits are strongly linked with how positive or negative our mood is likely to be at any given moment, or how likely we are to judge our life satisfactory or unsatisfactory.

Making the face fit

Another useful measure of happy emotion is to present people with a row of simply drawn faces—running the full range from elated to very depressed—and ask them to select the one that best reflects their mood. In 1976, Frank Andrews and Stephen Withey, working at the University of Michigan, reported on a large national U.S. survey that used just such a selection of faces, similar to the illustration below. In this survey, nearly half of the people questioned chose a pretty happy face as typical of their mood. Most of the others chose either an elated face or one that was slightly cheery. Very few people were prepared to admit to being below the neutral face toward the middle of the scale.

Negative emotions

According to one count, there have been seventeen times as many papers on depression as on happiness. If happiness is simply the opposite of depression, then we don't need to study it—it has all been done before. However, Norman Bradburn found that positive and negative emotions were not the opposite of one another; according to him they were independent.

Later research has shown that depression and happiness are, in fact, "negatively correlated"—those who experience positive emotions are less likely to experience negative emotions. They are also partly independent, though. A lot of negative emotion centers on the presence of things that bother or distress us—such as a neighbor's loud music—rather than always centering on the absence of things that would make us happy—such as an invitation to the party next door. In this way, a low score for negative emotion can, in many cases, be a useful indicator of happiness.

Well-documented causes of a disposition toward positive feelings are being an extrovert, being educated, being in employment, participating socially, experiencing positive life events (such as being promoted), and enjoying satisfying leisure time. Well-documented causes of a disposition towards negative emotion are having a neurotic, chiefly emotional personality, having low social status, being in poor health, having low self-esteem, and being in the midst of a stressful life-event (such as the death of someone close).

The extrovert personality

Extroversion is one of the most important human personality traits, in that it correlates with a wide range of behavior, including happiness. Although used by Jung in a slightly different way, the term is now taken to mean sociability, a desire for social interaction and for fostering relationships. Extroverts are also more likely to be impulsive risk-takers and sensation-seekers. Broadly, the introvert, someone who is very low in the extroversion scale, is seen as an altogether far quieter, more careful, and reserved kind of person.

Extroversion can be measured by questionnaires that ask people, for example, how much they enjoy talking to strangers, or whether they would prefer spending a quiet evening at home or going out to a party. After one long-term study, Paul Costa and colleagues at the American National Institutes of Health reported in 1981 that people who had scored high in extroversion scored high in happiness assessments seventeen years later. There are several possible explanations for the happiness of extroverts. In 1982, Jeffrey Gray, then working at the University of Oxford, England, proposed that extroverts are selective in the way that they receive feedback from those around them. Compared to introverts, extroverts are more sensitive to rewarding, reinforcing reactions from other people, and are less sensitive to negative, critical feedback.

Michael Argyle and colleagues at Oxford have found that there is a tendency for extroverts to have better social skills, such as assertiveness and cooperativeness, and that this may well explain their happiness. The direct correlation between extroversion and happiness is only moderately strong—other factors, such as assertiveness, also play a strong role. In other words, extroversion promotes happiness by promoting assertiveness.

Argyle has also found that extroverts have different leisure activities from introverts. They are more likely to belong to teams and clubs, and have a tendency to enjoy lively parties—and all these activities tend to make them happy.

Measuring satisfaction

Another part of what most people understand by happiness is satisfaction, and this is also a factor used by psychologists researching happiness. Satisfaction is not so much an emotion, but more a reflective judgement. One way psychologists have of measuring this is simply to ask: "How satisfied are you with your life as a whole?" Alternatively, they may use longer questionnaires, asking people how satisfied they are with the main areas of life that are seen as typical sources of satisfaction: work, personal relationships, and so on.

Another test of satisfaction is the ladder scale, designed in the 1960s by Hadley Cantril while working at Princeton University. With this test, people are asked to place themselves somewhere between the top and bottom of a ladder with nine rungs. Nearly everyone will choose a rung in the upper half. Participants were told that the top rung represents "the best possible life" and the bottom rung "the worst possible life." Most people chose rung six or seven.

The results produced by these different methods correlate well with each other—that is, individuals who are satisfied with one particular area of their lives are more likely to be satisfied with life as a whole. They also correlate well with measures of positive and negative emotions: People who judge that their lives are satisfactory tend to be in a better mood at any given time than people who judge their lives to be unsatisfactory.

So, psychologists making overall assessments of happiness have three useful components to take into consideration: degrees of positive emotion, of negative emotion, and of life satisfaction.

However, because extroversion and happiness are not perfectly correlated—that is to say, being happy does not guarantee being extroverted—there will be some happy introverts. When these introverts were identified and studied, they were happy because they scored strongly on other aspects of personality related to happiness, such as being low in neuroticism.

The neurotic personality

Your level of neuroticism (where you fit on a scale from unemotional to highly emotional) is another major personality trait. Psychologists measure it by using questionnaires that ask questions, for example, about how often you feel anxious or depressed. In a 1998 analysis, Kristina DeNeve and Harris Cooper, working at the Universities of Baylor and Missouri, reported on seventy-four studies of the relation between happiness and neuroticism that matched high neuroticism with low happiness. They found that neuroticism scores had a stronger overall correlation with happiness scores than extroversion scores had.

The explanation behind neurotics' unhappiness is not hard to find. In the first place, neuroticism is composed of a tendency toward depression,

Are women happier than men?

When it comes to happiness scores, very little difference has been found between men and women, though women, on average, are slightly happier when asked about their emotions. Women are also about twice as likely to say they are depressed—further evidence that happiness and unhappiness are not quite the opposite of each other—though the depressed are a minority and may not affect the overall average much. Also, the intensity of emotions, both positive and negative, is greater for women.

There are several reasons for more women than men saying that they feel depressed, and one of these is a difference in coping styles between the genders. Susan Nolen-Hoeksema, of the University of California, reported in 1991 that women tend to ruminate on their problems and that this does not appear to help them. Men, on the other hand, turn to physical activity and other kinds of distraction, and research has shown repeatedly how good exercise is for promoting positive moods.

Physical attractiveness and not being what they perceive as overweight is also important to women's happiness, as are family, children, and social relationships. Men, on the other hand, depend more on their jobs for satisfaction.

anxiety, emotional instability, a low stress threshold, and negative emotional states in general. In addition to this, those who are high in neuroticism have more negative experiences at work and leisure. This is partly a result of their negative emotions, and partly because they are not as rewarding company as extroverts and have fewer social skills.

"Manic" personalities are very interesting, since they appear to be very happy but are actually mentally disturbed. In a sense they really are very happy, though it may be more accurate to say that they are highly aroused or excited—as typically shown by their loud voices, incessant joking, and continuous talking.

A sense of control

"Control" as a dimension of personality was introduced in 1966 by Julian Rotter, working at the University of Connecticut. Rotter called it "internal control" and defined it as a person's generalized expectancy that they can control events rather than be controlled by others, or by luck or fate. This has been correlated with happiness, and it seems to be independent of other traits that correlate with happiness. Control can also be seen as the opposite of "learned helplessness," a state found in depressed people who feel that they are unable to influence what happens to them.

Depressed people often have a negative style of assessing their prospects and attributing blame—they believe that bad things will continue to happen to them and that these will be their own fault. Happy people think the opposite—that good things will continue to happen and that they are responsible for them. In 1997, Luo Lu and colleagues at the Kaosiung Medical College in Taiwan reported that a sense of control correlated with happiness, after extroversion, neuroticism, and demographic factors had been accounted for.

There are also class differences in control. People in "non-professional" classes feel they have less control over their lives and that there are greater constraints on them. This probably reflects their real-life experience, and it is part of the explanation for class differences in happiness. In 1998, Margie Lachman and Suzanne Weaver, working at Brandeis University, reported that a sense of mastery tended to correlate with positive scores for life satisfaction, good health, and low depression levels. The correlation was particularly strong for those on low incomes, where people's lack of a sense of control can help to explain their lower satisfaction levels and greater depression. Control also affects job satisfaction. Quite understandably, workers enjoy their work more if they feel they are free to do it as they want, and they do not enjoy being closely constrained.

Optimism—just "positive illusions"?

Optimism can be seen as another stable aspect of personality. It can be measured by testing people for a generalized positive expectancy about future events. It correlates strongly with individuals' happiness levels. It also correlates with health and the state of the immune system. In fact, most people are optimistic in their expectations. Some, however, are very optimistic, and can be said to have "positive illusions"—for example, they think that their future health is going to be much better than that of other similar people. In 1988, Shelley Taylor and Jonathon Brown, working at California and Southern Methodist Universities, argued that such positive illusions are good for us—they lead to positive self-evaluations, create optimism, and strengthen our sense of control. There is evidence that those with such positive illusions are happier, though people may find that a more successful strategy is to be realistic at the point of making decisions, and save optimism to use as an aid to carrying out decisions.

A sense of humor

There are consistent differences in how much people appreciate humor, how humorous they are themselves, and their use of it as a method of coping. Having a good sense of humor correlates with higher scores for happiness, and lower scores for depression and extroversion. One reason for this is that humor produces enjoyment of social situations, and enhances social bonding. Having a good sense of humor has also been found to work as a successful buffer against stress. It operates as a kind of optimism because it consists of being able to "see the funny side of things"—being able to see another less serious and less threatening side of negative events. Humor arises from being able to entertain two incongruous views at the same time.

The Pollyanna principle

Happy people are optimistic and have other positive biases, such as remembering only good things about the past. This has been described as the "Pollyanna principle," after the little girl in the early twentieth-century novel who always looked on the bright side. Happy people think well of themselves. They have high self-esteem and also think well of their friends. It might be thought that it would be best to strive for accurate judgements about all these things, but happy people do not, and this is part of the happy condition.

An audience in the 1940s laughing in a cinema.

The role of self-esteem

Self-esteem can be measured by questionnaires that ask people to agree or disagree with statements such as: "On the whole I am satisfied with myself." It has a high correlation with happiness. In fact, the relation is so close that it may be better to regard self-esteem as part of satisfaction—that is, satisfaction with the self.

Self-esteem is based partly on actual success, such as academic success, and it does correlate strongly with marks at school. In 1991, Hazel Markus and Shinobu Kitayama reported that this is not the case in "collectivist" cultures such as China and Korea, where there is a strong tradition of individuals working together and of viewing personal goals as less important than those of their family, friends, or work colleagues. Self-esteem in this type of culture depends more on the success of the group than on individual achievement.

Goals, meaning, and purpose

Having goals in life can give people a sense of meaning and purpose. The Austrian psychiatrist Viktor Frankl (1905–98) is famous not just for surviving four Nazi concentration camps, including Auschwitz, but also for helping others to do the same, by encouraging them to focus on worthwhile goals. Examples of such goals might be writing a book, or looking after someone.

Frankl—who held posts both in Vienna and the USA—later made this into a form of psychological therapy that he called logotherapy, from the Greek word *logos*, which can be translated as "meaning." Other therapists have reported the unhappiness and empty feelings of those who are rich in material things but who have no aim in life. Meaning and purpose can be measured by questionnaires that ask to what extent you have such goals and how far they have been fulfilled.

Goals enhance well-being in several ways. They give a sense of purpose, they give structure and meaning to daily life, they help people deal with problems and adversity, and they strengthen relationships with other people. In 1999, Nancy Cantor and Catherine Sanderson argued that goals have the greatest effect on well-being when they are (1) freely chosen, (2) realistic and likely to be achieved, (3) consistent with one another, and (4) when people can spend a lot of time in goal-related activities. Goals are, in a sense, part of the self; even if they have not been attained, they are still a distinctive part of an individual's personality.

There is another theory about goals and their effect on happiness, which seems at first to contradict what has been said so far. In 1985, Alex Michalos, working at the University of British Columbia, proposed that the gap between aspirations and actual achievements—the "goal-achievement gap"—is, in fact, a source of unhappiness. However, the two approaches are not really contradictory, since, as Cantor and Sanderson noted, it is important that goals should be realistic—that is, it should be possible, even likely, that they will be attained.

The resourceful personality

Resources such as money, education, and physical attractiveness make the attainment of certain goals possible, but some features of personality can also be seen as very useful resources. Intelligence has rather a small correlation with well-being, suggesting that other abilities may be more important. Social skills are a case in point. Extroverts have social skills that enable them to enjoy their social life more. One of the most important social skills is being rewarding company. The ability to handle people well is also important in all kinds of work situations.

It is worth noting that resources of any type affect well-being only if they are relevant to the goals that people seek. So, money is an important resource only for those who want to be rich or who have expensive tastes.

Nature and nurture

Some of the personality traits with which happiness is closely correlated, such as high extroversion and low neuroticism, are partly innate and do not change much. Our genes are to some degree responsible for our level of happiness. This is shown by twin studies—such as that carried out by David Lykken and Auke Tellegen, working at the University of Minnesota in 1988. They found that the happiness levels of identical twins were quite similar, while there was very little similarity for non-identical twins.

However, a happy outlook is also affected by environmental experiences. For example, positive experiences with leisure groups and at work leads to increased happiness over long periods of time. Happiness is a joint effect of personality and the environment, even though personality has a greater effect. And there is interaction between the two. For example, people can choose or avoid aspects of their environment on the basis of what makes them feel good or bad.

The next two chapters look more closely at the impact on happiness of demographic variables such as age, sex, class, and so on, resources such as personal wealth or an attractive appearance, and lifestyle choices such as the cultivation of relationships or the way we use our leisure time.

12: managing good and bad fortune David Nias

Opportunities for happiness

Though fortune's malice
overthrow my state,
My mind exceeds the
compass of her wheel **William Shakespeare**

Happiness around the world: a group of cheerful children in Yemen.

If it's happiness that you want from life, then, to some extent, you will need luck—and one of the best pieces of luck possible is to have a happy disposition. Chapter 11 has shown how deeply rooted in personality are a person's mood and their readiness to judge that their life is satisfactory. This chapter looks at factors other than personality. How much influence do the events of our lives have on our happiness? What is the effect of the circumstances we live in? What difference does it make how we choose to live?

Going beyond your personality

Some people always seem to be cheerful, or at least contented, regardless of what happens. Other people seem perpetually gloomy. An exception are those who suffer from mood swings—miserable one day and joyfully happy the next (manic-depressives represent an extreme form of this tendency toward cycles of mood).

This is why many events that would gladden or torment most people at the time have surprisingly little effect on long-term happiness. Someone with a generally happy disposition will still feel pain and grief when a serious misfortune occurs, and you would have to be exceptionally dour not to get an initial thrill from winning a million in the lottery. However, once you get used to your new circumstances, you will probably feel more or less as satisfied (or discontented) as before.

Escape from material deprivation makes those with very little money happier, regardless of their general disposition. However, when people already have even a modest amount of money, though they may feel pleased to get a salary increase or win the lottery, extra wealth makes very little difference to their long-term happiness. Similarly, people living in countries where hot, sunny days are not a novelty—and probably precisely because this is no novelty—do not seem any happier than those in cooler climes, to whom a warm, sunny day will bring an instant mood-lift.

Nevertheless, you can be more happy or less happy in the long run, depending on what your life brings you and the choices that you make about how to respond. Roughly speaking, the main areas of experience that really matter are the same as those identified by Sigmund Freud early in the twentieth century as the keys to good mental health: love, work, and play.

Coping with disaster

Being born with physical disabilities or acquiring them as a result of a serious accident provides an obvious example of how people's lives could potentially be wrecked. Despite the increasing availability of aids, people's lives may still be severely limited. It is therefore natural to assume that disabled people feel sad for much of the time, because they are comparing themselves with others.

Research indicates that, on first becoming physically disabled, people are very unhappy for several months, but then recover to a large extent. The main studies in this area were carried out in the 1970s by Philip Brickman (at Northwestern University) and colleagues, and in the 1980s by Richard Schulz (University of Pittsburgh), and Susan Decker (University of Portland's School of Nursing).

These researchers interviewed people who had become paralyzed as a result of serious accidents. For most of them, happiness eventually rose towards its usual level. It seems that, once people adjust to such a tragedy, their expectations change and they become about as content with their reduced advantages as they were with their better advantages before the accident. Most of the people interviewed claimed they were "almost as happy" as they were before. Surveys have also found that physically disabled people as a group are surprisingly close to the population average for self-reported happiness.

However, this is not to say that certain physical conditions, such as those that are associated with chronic pain or lack of energy, do not cause great ongoing unhappiness. Indeed, terminal illness, especially in old age, is one of the main causes of suicide.

Winning a fortune

"Common sense" might tell us that having money creates happiness, and it is all too obvious that not having any money creates real problems. However, research on the effects of winning a fortune indicates that the popular view that it solves many of life's problems is wrong.

When people are asked if being better off financially would make them happier, nearly everyone agrees that it would. Typically they say that the ability to buy almost anything one wants without needing to worry is obviously a desirable state of affairs. But interviews with the winners of huge cash prizes reveal that a temporary euphoria surrounding the win soon gives way to worry about the problems of everyday life. Apart from buying a better house and car, most invest the money for the future. As a result, their everyday spending is affected very little. And if they give up work and move away from their friends, the familiar and comfortable landmarks of their normal lifestyle may disappear, causing matters to take a turn for the worse.

In a U.K. study from the 1970s, people who had won a large prize in English soccer sweepstakes were contacted by researchers Stephen Smith and Peter Razzell. A total of 191 winners agreed to be interviewed a year or more after their win. As expected, they had moved to better houses, had acquired better cars, and were taking more exotic vacations. Apart from an increase in headaches, they also seemed in better health.

However, not everything was to the pools winners' advantage. A common complaint was that they were being pestered for money. Because of the publicity surrounding their win, they were constantly being asked for donations to charitable and not-so-charitable causes. Another common complaint was the envy of neighbors, friends, and relatives. Perhaps because of these changes for the worse, they rated themselves as "no happier" than they had been before their win.

Those pools winners who chose to move to a better house in a new area were likely to experience loneliness. Often their new neighbors would adopt a snobbish attitude towards them. About 70 percent of the winners gave up work as a result of their win. Because work is often a source of friendship, this too led to an increase in loneliness.

Similar findings to these have been obtained in other studies, such as past winners of the Illinois State Lottery, who were found to be no happier than non-winners. Even a comparison of lottery winners with people who have been badly paralyzed in accidents revealed no clear difference in happiness when interviews were conducted a year after the win or accident.

The role of religious faith

There is a small positive correlation between happiness and being a church member or a religious believer. In a study published in 1965, David Moberg and Marvin Taves found that the effect is greater for old people, and the main reason is the strong social support of church communities.

Two other processes come into this area: (1) feeling close to God and engaging in private prayer, which works in some ways like other relationships, and (2) having firm beliefs. In 1989, Melvin Pollner, working at the University of California at Los Angeles, and Christopher Ellison and colleagues at Duke University, reported that these processes operate independently from simply being a believer or a church member. They have a stronger effect on a narrower area of happiness—"existential well-being"—by which is meant having a satisfactory relation with God and a purpose in life. Religious services are also a source of strong positive emotions, and this contributes to the positivity component of happiness.

When it comes to being a church member, this seems to have a stronger effect on health than the other factors, and we've seen that good health and happiness are correlated. Robert Hummer and colleagues, working at the University of Texas at Austin, reported in 1999 on a demographic study of 22,000 Americans over a period of eight years. They concluded that church membership added seven years to life expectancy. The main reason is the better health-related behavior of church members as opposed to non-members—such as less smoking, drinking, and promiscuous sex—though social support also affects health and church membership can often supply an element of this.

Mental health is also related to having a form of religious belief. This is partly because religion buffers stress, especially uncontrollable life events such as bereavement, so that these stresses do less damage. In 1996, Crystal Park and colleagues at the University of California found that religious people were less depressed after experiencing stress. The suicide rate of church members is about a quarter that of non-members, and there is less fear of death.

Michael Argyle

Does money buy happiness?

It is widely believed that money can make us happy, which is why so many people enter lotteries. In fact, in well-off countries, the correlation between satisfaction and income is very small, in spite of the vast range of tempting goods that it can buy. Perhaps the reason for this is that, from middle incomes upward, what people spend their money on—jewelry or larger cars and houses, for example—no longer meets important needs.

However, money can give another satisfaction: a sense of higher status through comparing oneself favorably with others. Job satisfaction is higher for those who earn above the average compared with people of similar occupation, education, and age.

Money has a greater effect at the lower end of the income scale, and in poorer countries such as Turkey, Slovenia, and Estonia. To people who need to spend the next bit of money they get on food and other basic necessities, it matters much more whether they obtain that money than it does for higher-income people. Depression is greater for the poor, who worry more about money problems and have no financial resources to deal with any crises. Health is worse too, because low-income groups have poorer nutrition and hygiene, and do not take as much care of themselves as those with more money. Their health also suffers because their low status in society means that they have poor morale.

Do increases in income make people happier? For a time, yes, in the case of salary rises, but people soon get used to the new salary, and return to their previous level of happiness. The satisfaction gained from an increase in income is not as great as the satisfaction gained by earning more than people who are similar to oneself.

There have been large changes in income over time: Americans earn four times more per head now than in 1970, but there has been no increase in life satisfaction at all. The explanation may be that people's expectations and aspirations have also steadily increased over time. Where once they wanted a small car and a radio, they now want several cars and TV sets.

Michael Argyle

How important are class and education?

In 1994, Ruut Veenhoven and colleagues at the University of Rotterdam published a three-volume compilation of surveys from around the world. It included evidence of quite a strong relation between happiness and social class—measured, for example, by occupational status or income.

The effect of class has become smaller in recent American studies, but is much stronger in some other countries, such as Nigeria, India, and Brazil—all countries where there is a very unequal income distribution, and a lot of very poor people. One of the reasons for this effect of class on happiness is that people of higher social status are richer and can satisfy their material needs better—we have already seen that income may have a weak overall effect, but it has a much stronger one at the lower end of the income scale. Middle-class people also take part in more leisure activities, have more satisfying jobs and stronger social networks, and enjoy more respect from others, and all these things contribute to their happiness.

There is a positive link between level of education and happiness. The main explanation is that education leads to better jobs and higher incomes. When job status and income are held constant, education has a smaller effect. However, education has a much stronger effect in certain countries, including Japan, Singapore, Korea, and Mexico—presumably because education gives greater advantages there than in other places.

In 1977, Catherine Ross and Marieke Van Willigen of Ohio State and East Carolina Universities reported that education leads to more satisfying jobs, greater internal control, better leisure and "inner" life, and more access to forms of social support.

Michael Argyle

Is one nationality happier than another?

Surveys undertaken in different countries using various measures of happiness have provided some interesting—and sometimes puzzling—results. Research into national differences has been pioneered by Richard Lynn, working at the New University of Ulster in Northern Ireland, from the 1970s onwards. He has found that Americans tend to report the highest levels of happiness while people living in China and Japan report the lowest levels.

In a comparison of eight European countries based on Lynn's results, Italy came last when people were asked directly how happy and satisfied they were. Closer inspection of the results, however, revealed something interesting. While coming last on "happiness" and "satisfaction with life," Italy was near the middle on an index based on its levels of divorce, alcoholism, and crime—which statistical studies have linked with unhappiness—and was almost the best country for having a low suicide rate. This discrepancy between different levels of happiness can be partly explained in terms of happiness and unhappiness not being exact opposites (see also previous chapter).

Other interesting results from this European survey include Denmark coming top for "satisfaction with life," but having the worst suicide rate (over five times higher than in Italy). France is worst off for "divorce, alcoholism, and crime," but is average on the other measures. When happiness and unhappiness are averaged, however, there are not that many differences among the eight countries.

The value of friendship

Apart from personality, friendship is a much clearer source of long-term happiness than any other we have discussed so far. And it seems even more important for women than it is for men. Women tend to form friendships that are closer and more intimate, and they are more likely to confide in their friends than are men. They are also more likely than men to seek the company of others when feeling depressed or upset.

When they are socializing with friends, people are usually in a positive mood. This is partly because of the enjoyable things they do together, partly because of the positive verbal and non-verbal messages exchanged. Michael Argyle's research team at Oxford, England, has found that leisure activities that involve belonging to teams and clubs, and going to lively parties and dances, provide more happiness than other leisure activities. One way in which friends, partners, and relatives can make us happy is by being in a good mood themselves. This contagious quality of mood was demonstrated in a classic psychology study reported in 1969 by Stanley Schachter of Columbia University.

Possible causes of national differences

If there are any national differences in happiness, what are the causes? From the self-report surveys that have been done, the main factors that correlate with happiness are: wealth (average national income shows rather a strong statistical association with average national happiness—in other words, richer countries are happier); equality of incomes (though this correlation is greater in richer countries); good human rights situation, existence of democratic institutions, trust in government, and political stability. Individualism also correlates with happiness, though only for rich countries and when single-item measures are used. However, if we use objective indicators, then collectivist countries (cultures such as China and Japan, where the success of the group is more important than that of the individual) do well—an issue that was touched on in the last chapter. Because of their high level of social support, such cultures have much lower rates of suicide, heart disease, mental illness, and alcoholism. The negative side of collectivism, however, is the loss of freedom from control by the family.

In recent surveys, the U.S.A., Australia, Scandinavia, Iceland, and Switzerland score high on reported happiness. Italy, France, and the rest of Europe come out surprisingly low. It seems odd that 45 percent of Danes are very happy, but only 5 percent of Italians are. These results are based on the replies to a single question, of the kind "How satisfied are you with your life?"

If we take extroversion and neuroticism as indirect measures of happiness and unhappiness respectively, then the low scores for Europe disappear. On this measure of happiness, India and Nigeria come out top, though China and Russia still come out low.

What may be happening in surveys that address just one aspect or issue is that various national biases in self-presentation have crept in. For example, there is plenty of evidence that American people, especially young people, think that they are supposed to be happy. They give happier responses in interviews than in questionnaires, and if asked single, broad questions rather than a series of specific ones.

Another approach to measuring national differences is by using "objective" social indicators for unhappiness such as suicide, alcoholism, divorce, unemployment, ill health, and crime. Because these factors have been shown to correlate with unhappiness, their levels in any given country are often used as indicators of that country's general level of unhappiness. (There are no corresponding measures for happiness as yet, though percentages of families who stay together and use of leisure facilities are possibilities.) However, a hazard of this technique is that different countries have different cultures for recording such statistics. For example, coroners may be more reluctant to classify deaths as suicide in countries where there is a greater stigma against suicide (such as Roman Catholic Italy or France) than in others (such as Scandinavia).

Michael Argyle

In this study, volunteers were given a stimulant drug (adrenaline) before waiting—along with another person—to be assessed for mood. If their companion acted in a happy way (emphasizing the joys of being a student, for example), their mood was likely to change in this direction. Similarly, if their companion acted in an angry way (say, showing resentment at being a "guinea pig" or at being kept waiting), their mood was likely to change to one of anger. Apart from illustrating the general enhancing effects of adrenaline on mood, this study is cited to demonstrate how easily we can be influenced by the mood of those around us.

Following a study in a tenpin bowling club, Robert Kraut and Robert Johnston, of Cornell University, reported in 1979 on an interaction between friendship and happy smiling. The bowlers smiled much more at each other, rather than at the pines, regardless of whether they had scored a hit or a miss. This shows the importance of friends—we are far more likely to smile and be happy when we are in a social situation. A similar result was observed when studying people in the street. Although people on their own are more likely to smile when it is sunny rather than cloudy, most people will smile when they are with companions, whatever the weather.

Olympic gold-medal-winners provide an example of extreme happiness. In 1995, José-Miguel Fernandez-Dols and Maria-Angeles Ruiz-Belda, of the University of Madrid, reported on their observations of the medal-winners during the awards ceremonies at the Olympic Games in Barcelona. For most of the time they appeared very serious, smiling only when interacting with the spectators. Intense happiness on its own was not sufficient for smiling. Again it is the social situation that is important.

An important series of studies—pioneered in the 1970s by George Brown and Tirril Harris, of the University of London, England—has pointed to the protective role of intimate friends in guarding against depression. People are especially vulnerable to depression if they lack a close companion. Housewives living in blocks of flats with several young children are repeatedly found to be at risk of depression if they lack close friends in whom they can confide. One problem is that, if they are depressed, then they are likely to repel potential friends, which in turn increases their depressed mood. Skilled befriending of vulnerable people can act to prevent or relieve depression.

Friends, good company, captured in *The Luncheon of the Boating Party*, 1881, by Renoir.

The beautiful people

Being attractive is an advantage when you are initiating social contacts (which we've seen contribute to well-being), and beautiful women in particular often claim to feel especially happy. In the 1970s, in order to check on this observation, Eugene Mathes and Arnold Kahn asked students at Iowa State University to rate their own happiness, self-esteem, and mental health. Independent judges rated the students for physical attractiveness. Although it is often said that "beauty is in the eye of the beholder," people in fact agree remarkably well on who is attractive.

The results showed that there was a slight but consistent trend for attractive female students to report greater happiness and more positive feelings about themselves. The same trend did not apply to male students, perhaps because society places less value on men's looks. (There has been much talk recently of men becoming more preoccupied with their appearance, but research to date does not suggest that this is having a significant overall effect as yet on society's attitudes.)

Attractive couples also seem to have an advantage when it comes to happiness. In an early study (published in 1951), Clifford Kirkpatrick and John Cotton asked students at Indiana University to identify well-adjusted and poorly adjusted couples among their friends and acquaintances.

Interviewers then visited the couples and rated them for physical attractiveness. The well-adjusted group had a preponderance of attractive people. It also seemed that the attractiveness of the wife was more important to a happy marriage than that of the husband. Although the well-adjusted partners were usually similar in attractiveness, it was the wife who was likely to be the better-looking if there was a discrepancy.

What does this finding mean? Perhaps when working to make a marriage happy, a woman will also work to improve her appearance by diet, exercise, and smart clothes—and this is what the interviewers noticed. It might be expected that things have changed somewhat since this 1950s study, but research undertaken since then has continued to support its findings.

Paul Newman and Joanne Woodward, pictured in 1961: people who are roughly equal in physical attractiveness tend to pair off. Then begins a complicated process of exploring each other's personalities—to discover whether they can make each other happy.

What happens when physical charms begin to fade? One of the ways we view our current level of happiness is by comparison with what we experienced in the past. When our looks fade, we might suppose that we may become less happy. In 1975, Ellen Berscheid and Elaine Walster, working at the Universities of Minnesota and Wisconsin respectively, reported on a study comparing the happiness and looks of middle-aged people with how they were as students. College yearbooks provided photographs of them when they were young. Women who were very attractive when young tended to be less happy and less well-adjusted by the time they reached fifty years of age. No such relationship was found for men—probably as male looks are seen to be less important in our society.

Love and marriage

We are always hearing about the distress caused by marital disharmony and divorce. Many marriages end in divorce, with much associated grief and anger. Even with happy marriages, the freedom of the partners is curtailed and each is likely to make demands on the other. It is sometimes argued that marriage as an institution has outlived its usefulness, and we would be better off without it. On the other hand, having a close, long-term, stable relationship with another person is usually seen as forming the basis of true happiness.

Research indicates that most couples tend to be happier married than they would be on their own (some studies define married as meaning those with a certificate, while others include cohabiting partners along with married couples). Indeed, living with a compatible partner is likely to be a source of great happiness. Surveys repeatedly find that married people tend to be happier than single or divorced people. In 1981, Joseph Veroff and colleagues at the University of Michigan reported on a nationally representative American survey. Far higher percentages of married men, and especially women, claimed to be "very happy" compared with single and divorced people.

Contrary to traditional folklore, it appears that it is men rather than women who most need marriage. In several ways, men get more from marriage and so feel its loss more acutely when it breaks down. When couples split up, it is the men who are most likely to become depressed and even ill. This may be because women tend to be much better at providing companionship and social support, and so the men have more to lose. Or it could be because men need someone to look after them! Whatever the explanation, the finding is that men are the ones who most desire and then appreciate marriage.

Investigations into the causes of marital disharmony suggest that it is the attitude of the wife that is most important in determining the happiness of both partners. Women with (for want of a better word) "feminist" attitudes are believed to experience problems because they tend to confront their partner when there is conflict of interests. At the other extreme, "traditional" women are believed to experience problems because they tend to use techniques such as "emotional manipulation" when a conflict arises. Surveys found the happiest wives to be those who tread a middle path between these two extremes. Rather than confronting, manipulating, or giving in, they tend to use the negotiating technique of give and take in their relationships.

The truth behind the slogan: "The family that plays together, stays together" is indicated by evidence from a study of 200 couples. Those pursuing joint or shared interests expressed a greater degree of marital satisfaction than did those pursuing parallel activities. Worst off were

Rousseau's *Wedding Party* presents a dreamlike version of the day of marriage.

those involved in individual or solitary activities. This finding could mean that couples with shared interests are going to be happier, or that making efforts to cultivate similar interests will enhance a marriage. There is probably an element of truth in both explanations.

On balance, the evidence indicates strongly that marriage is good for us, even if there are many notable exceptions. As well as finding greater happiness in married than in single people, married people tend to be healthier and to live longer. Even divorced people choose to marry again, often very soon afterwards.

Marriage and mental health

While it lasts, romantic love induces intense joy, partly due to sexual arousal, partly due to adoration by the other. Studies suggest that marriage produces the most enduring happiness—because of the help, emotional support, and companionship provided by the partner. Of course, some marriages are unhappy, and many break up. And the ending of a marriage—by divorce, separation, or death—is also very distressing. (In a similar way, just as children can be a source of great joy, they can also cause great distress at certain stages, especially as babies and adolescents.)

However, marriage in particular appears to buffer the effect of stress on mental health. The rate of mental hospital admission is lowest for the married, most for the divorced. The causal effect of marriage on mental health has been shown in a study reported by Allan Horwitz and colleagues at Rutgers University, New Jersey, in 1996. They followed up a number of initially unmarried individuals for seven years. Those who got married showed a fall in depression and alcoholism compared with those who remained single. A study comparing marriage with cohabiting showed greater happiness among the married couples.

Health is also greatly affected by social support. Lisa Berkman and Leonard Syme, of Yale and the University of California, Berkeley, followed up 7,000 Americans for nine years in the 1970s. The numbers who died during this period were much lower for those who were married and were members of other groups and networks.

According to Bert Uchino and colleagues at the University of Utah and Ohio State University, reporting in 1996, the main reasons for these effects on health are that social support activates the immune and other biological systems. This effect is more important than the other beneficial process associated with close relationships: the tendency of those in them to take better care of their health.

Michael Argyle

Children—a source of happiness?

It is often assumed that a marriage is not complete without children. For many people, the main reason for getting married is to have children. If children fail to arrive, there is often great sadness. Moreover, most couples do not stop at having one child; two or three is usually seen as the optimum number. It is, therefore, natural to assume that most people look forward with eager anticipation to the arrival of children.

But the reality is that children can cause a lot of problems, if not actual stress, especially at certain stages of development. This can more than cancel out the joys of having children. The main studies in this area were started in the 1970s—by Elmer Spreitzer and Eldon Snyder, working at Bowling Green State University, and by Angus Campbell and colleagues working at the University of Michigan. Their surveys found that couples without children tended to be the happiest.

Similarly, married couples remembered being happier before their children arrived. This reduction in happiness at the child-rearing stage is more apparent for women than it is for men. This is most probably because it is the woman who makes most of the sacrifices necessary to look after children.

Consistent with these findings, couples become happier again as the children grow up. Perhaps this is partly because they have more time for each other. There also tends to be an increase in a couple's happiness when the children finally leave home. At this turning point in their life, couples are forced to restructure their lifestyle. This may lead to a more interesting life in which they form new friendships and develop new interests and pastimes.

An alternative interpretation is that happiness ratings are higher, not because they are free from looking after their children, but because of the change in lifestyle (the "a change is as good as a rest" scenario).

Because of the above evidence that children are not always a source of happiness, we need to think of ways in which family life might be improved. In the recent past, when large, extended families were more common, there were several people who could share in the tasks of looking after and playing with the children. Perhaps it is the gradual move away from extended families, leaving just the couple to shoulder all the responsibility, that is the cause of the stress and strain that is so often apparent these days.

The rewards of work

Most of us spend a third of the day at work—the other two-thirds being taken up by sleep and leisure. Because of this, it is important that we enjoy our work and there are, in fact, many ways in which it can contribute to happiness. There is the satisfaction of a job well done and of the reward of promotion to look forward to: a job gives a sense of status and purpose. Most jobs also involve a number of social contacts and benefits that extend beyond the workplace. Having a consistent structure to the day is also important.

We all need something to look forward to in the course of our working day. Coffee and tea breaks are particularly important, especially for those people who are doing monotonous work. Surveys have shown that having enjoyable breaks enhances job satisfaction and morale. Such breaks are best held away from the immediate work area, in a common room, for example.

Many people complain about boring or stressful work. But at least half the working population claim to be satisfied with their job. When questioned, about a third of people say they would continue to work even if they did not need the money. For example, one large American company needed to reduce its workforce temporarily. The company offered to pay for its staff to take a prolonged vacation for six months. After taking a real but short vacation, many of those involved admitted that they had taken other work because they felt ill at ease without a definite structure to the day.

Unemployed people as a group are usually far from happy. The warning signs of mental ill health, if not actual symptoms, become apparent following the loss of a job. It is certainly the case that work is most appreciated when we no longer have it! Because of the mental distress associated with the loss of a job, it is important for the unemployed to find a substitute, such as a new hobby.

Unemployment is a particular problem because many out-of-work people seem to "waste" their day. Surveys find that unemployed people rarely make good use of their new leisure time. For example, in one British government survey, 1,043 unemployed people were asked what they had done the day before. The most cited activities were rather mundane ones such as housework and shopping. An incidental finding was that unemployed people entertained less but smoked more. Losing a job lowers mood and this in turn reduces initiative, and so people do less and less.

What type of work is the most satisfying? Job satisfaction tends to be higher in the more technical and highly paid occupations. It is this work that is likely to be the most interesting and challenging, although there are many exceptions. Farmers, lawyers, and managers also give high ratings. Sales staff, clerical staff, and manual workers give relatively lower ratings. Unskilled workers usually give very low ratings, especially if their work is also stressful. People in boring jobs tend to be "clock watchers," looking forward to the end of the working day.

There is a tendency to find work more satisfying as we get older. A study combining the results of several surveys across the United States found an increase in job satisfaction right up to retirement age. This applied to both men and women. Surveys in other countries have found a decline earlier in people's working lives, but then a gradual increase in enthusiasm towards retirement. What a pity it is that people are forced to give up and retire, when they are at or near to their happiest time at work!

Growing old

There is a small increase in satisfaction and other aspects of happiness with age, especially for men. The effect of age is reduced if health, education, and similar variables are kept constant, but it is still there. Age effects are sometimes due to historical changes; perhaps everyone was happier when today's elderly people were young and they stayed that way. Increased satisfaction is a real effect of age—as shown by long-term studies such as that reported in 1998 by Ravenna Helson and Eva Lohnen of the University of California, where the same individuals have been tested at different ages.

This effect is surprising, since older people are likely to be in worse health, have reduced incomes, and be retired or widowed. The explanation is probably that aspirations are lower and the gap between aspirations and achievements has almost disappeared. If old people are retired or widowed, then so are their friends—this is what is normal. Another explanation is that older people adapt, by seeking out situations and other people that they enjoy most.

Various studies have shown satisfaction with work increasing steadily throughout our working lives, and satisfaction with income goes up with age, at least to retirement. Clark, Oswald, and Warr (at the University of New Orleans in 1996) found in a national study of 10,000 individuals that overall job satisfaction fell from age 16–19 to a low at age 31, after which it rose. Satisfaction with health, however, goes down, as does satisfaction with leisure.

Michael Argyle

Leisure pursuits and happiness

Having control over our life is a key to good mental health—and normally the area of our lives over which we have the most control is our leisure time. Many different needs can be met through leisure pursuits. We may need to relax, and so choose to do something tranquil like painting landscapes or meditating. Or we may need stimulation, in which case we might choose anything from playing in a jazz band to parachute jumping. Using leisure to gain new skills and knowledge that turn into a lifelong pursuit is one of the best ways to increase happiness. And if you are in control of your life, you can always switch to a new interest whenever you feel like it.

Some people deliberately choose something different from their work—mountaineering for an office worker, for example. More often, though, work spills over into leisure. Those in intellectual work, for example, often choose pursuits such as reading books or membership of a local history society in their spare time.

When people are asked which activities give them the most satisfaction, family life usually comes top, followed by social events. A nationally representative sample of over 1,000 Americans, undertaken in the 1970s by John Robinson of Maryland University, found that both work and leisure activities were related to overall quality of life, and that family life was the most important. Many more people chose this rather than watching television or going to clubs.

Going on vacation brings a stimulating change of scene, a relief from everyday pressures, and often increased activity and sociability. A more permanent strategy for better happiness is to build more activity and more social enjoyment into normal life.

When Joseph Veroff and colleagues at Michigan reported in 1981 on women aged sixty-five years and over, they found that their perceived life satisfaction, in the form of happiness and morale, was closely associated with an active life. These activities included common pastimes for this age-group, such as socializing with friends, organizing charity events, and going for walks. This association between happiness and an active life was even closer than it was for income or health. But it should be pointed out that poor health can greatly restrict participation in leisure activity.

The value of leisure activities

Leisure is one of the main causes of happiness and well-being generally, and it is the one that is simplest to change. Laboratory experiments into inducing certain moods in people show that it is easy to alter mood, though the change may not last long. However, in the 1980s, Robert Thayer, at California State University, Long Beach, asked subjects to go for a ten-minute brisk walk. This produced positive moods that lasted for over two hours. Similarly, the effects of energetic sport may last in some people until the following day. Sport and exercise have also been found to have a strong effect in reducing depression, and to a lesser extent anxiety, and so some enlightened doctors are now prescribing exercise for these conditions.

Forms of leisure that have been shown by research to have lasting effects on happiness and satisfaction include: commitment to exercise or sport, belonging to social clubs, doing voluntary work, attending church services, and other "serious" leisure activities (as opposed to simply watching TV).

Seppo Iso-Ahola and Crystal Park, of the Universities of Maryland and California, reported in 1996 that leisure groups—in which people engage in leisure together—buffer the effect of stress in producing depression. There is also a big effect on physical health: reducing the likelihood of heart attacks, for example. Although the unemployed have been shown to be unhappy, this has also been alleviated in field experiments providing sport facilities and training. The National Volunteering Center in London is encouraging the unemployed to do voluntary work, partly to enhance their well-being, partly to give them some work training.

Michael Argyle

When the sun is shining...

Many people are in a better mood when the weather is good—sunshine, moderate warmth, and low humidity. In 1983, Norbert Schwarz and Gerald Clore, working at the University of Heidelberg in Germany, reported that people rate themselves happier, and more satisfied with life as a whole, under such weather conditions. People are more likely to stop and volunteer to answer street surveys when the weather is sunny. They also tend to give higher tips in restaurants, even when they are dining indoors. There seems to be something naturally exhilarating about good weather that makes us happier, more helpful, and more generous.

Too much hot, sunny weather, however, can be a bad thing, and stifling heat is obviously distressing. People who live in sunny climates do not rate themselves as happier than people in cold and wet climates. It is probably the case that we adapt to the prevailing climate where we live and soon become bored if it is always the same. As with most things, what is needed is a bit of variety.

Water and the countryside also have a positive impact. People are more likely to report feeling happy when surrounded by wild, natural countryside or by water scenes. Also important is depth of view, since people like to be able to look across an expanse of countryside or water. It seems that Nature gives us a sense of peace and tranquillity, although the effect is more apparent in those visiting, rather than living in, such surroundings.

Taking a vacation

It is hardly surprising that people are happier when on vacation. An improvement in climate and diet are just two of the likely benefits. Both mental and physical health seem to improve. A study carried out in 1980 reported that minor symptoms (such as feeling tired) more than halve when people are on vacation.

Georges Seurat's 1884 painting, *Bathers at Asnieres,* reflecting the relaxing qualities of a day in the sun.

While we may not be able to take frequent vacations, we can at least make the most of our weekends. For example, taking advantage of good weekend weather by making sure that we go out, combined with hobbies and pastimes that we can pursue in the evenings, should help to benefit our mental and physical health.

In 1982, Philip Pearce of the University of North Queensland assessed vacationers on Brampton Island, near the Australian Barrier Reef, for problems such as headaches and insomnia. He contrasted the amount of time that people experienced various symptoms during their vacation compared with their past year. While such problems were common before the vacation, they tended to disappear after a few days by the sea.

What contributes most to happiness?

It can be seen that many aspects of life contribute to happiness, and chief among them are not those things that we might expect, such as material possessions and money. There is much truth in the song title: "The best things in life are free."

The most intense feelings of happiness arise, not surprisingly, from falling in love. Other happy events include getting married or engaged, having a child, going on vacation, completing a degree, and getting promoted at work.

In the long term, the most important areas are family life, followed by friendships, then work, and then leisure. In all of these areas, happiness results not simply by chance, but because we use social skills to build relationships and judge how best to take advantage of opportunities. As we have mentioned, leisure is precisely the area of life over which we have the most control, and therefore it is also the one in which we have the most opportunity to do something about enhancing our own happiness. It may be worth experimenting—to see, for example, whether a daily walk or some other exercise (at the expense, say, of time spent watching television) helps to boost your mood overall.

Meeting lower and higher needs

In the 1950s, the eminent American psychotherapist Abraham Maslow (1908–1970) argued that our needs can be ranked in an ascending order. The ones at the top can be achieved only if the basic ones have been met. He constructed a pyramid to illustrate this. At ground floor level are our basic physiological needs, such as hunger and thirst. Then comes safety and security needs. When these needs are met, our thoughts can turn to love and sex. At the next level is the need for self-esteem and achievement. And at the highest level are the "self-actualizing" needs, such as art and music.

It is claimed that people who reach this highest level lead lives filled with excitement and meaning. Someone who has good mental health, along with positive feelings about various aspects of their life, is said to be "self-actualized." A questionnaire called the Personal Orientation Inventory was designed to measure a person's degree of self-actualization or positive mental health. Here are some examples of the type of items involved: my spare time is full of interesting activities; I like to help others; my work is fun; I am in control of my life; my life is full of meaning; I have high moral principles.

The exceptional mental health of self-actualized people has been summarized in terms of six characteristics:

1. **Self-actualizers generate vitality.** Friends regard them as having dynamic or magnetic personalities. They are full of energy and enthusiasm; they work and play hard.
2. **They are both insightful and realistic.** There is a reflective side to the self-actualizing personality. Because of this they see the world for what it is, and so can be realistic in their judgments.
3. **They have a zest for living.** The theory is that having satisfied their basic needs, they have more energy available to pursue other interests. They live for the moment, taking each day as it comes. They are full of spontaneity and exuberance.
4. **They are individuals.** Thoughtful and enthusiastic, they conform only when they think it right. Their life is self-determined, and as such they are seen as individualistic.
5. **They are sensitive to the needs of others.** Perhaps because they have satisfied their own needs, they are free to care about others. They are characterized by empathy and warmth.
6. **They have peak experiences.** Because they are free to focus on the higher things in life, like freedom and beauty, they are more likely to find these elusive experiences.

Peak experiences

No account of happiness would be complete without reference to "peak experiences," claimed to be the highest form of happiness. These experiences are rare and may happen only a few times in a person's life, if they are lucky. These are moments of transcendence, of "being at one with the world," often with an underlying sense of euphoria, satisfaction, and contentment. Peak experiences must be distinguished from manic episodes. One of the main differences is that the mentally healthy person is relaxed and in control.

To test the assumption that the self-actualized person is the type most likely to have peak experiences, the Personal Orientation Inventory was given to a group of 222 people who had applied for permits to visit protected American wilderness areas. It was thought that these people, because of their interest in nature and the wild, would score high on self-actualization. And so it proved, with this group scoring higher than a group of 500 randomly selected adults.

In interviews, it emerged that the self-actualized were attracted to the wilderness because they found it aesthetically pleasing and physically challenging. Many of them described peak experiences they remembered from the past. In particular, it was aspects of nature that helped to create the opportunity for these greatly valued moments of transcendence.

13: strategies for happiness David Nias

Getting more out of life

Every day and in every way,
I'm getting better and better

Emil Coué

Besides analyzing happiness, psychologists have developed techniques for actually making people happy. The main thrust of this work has come from clinical psychologists trying to help people who are depressed. However, the therapeutic techniques they have developed for mood elevation and better satisfaction with life are worth anyone's attention. They not only help the ill and distressed; they can help an already well-adjusted person to live a happier life. This is different from most treatments, where you have to be ill to benefit. Unlike antidepressant medication—which is appropriate only for people who are seriously or chronically depressed—these techniques require active commitment and involvement on the part of the patient. Commitment and involvement are half the battle won.

Simple pleasures

Both direct and indirect strategies have roles to play in raising our mood. Direct approaches include relaxation and meditation, while taking a vacation is an example of an activity that can bring indirect benefits. Exercise helps us in both ways. It can lift mood directly, as a result of its physiological effects—such as increasing adrenaline and producing endorphins (the brain chemical that increases pleasure). It can also enhance mood indirectly, by improving our health and making us feel better about ourselves and our bodies—as well as adding a stimulating, enriching aspect to our lives and widening our social contacts, if our exercise activities involve meeting with other people.

Some pleasures are very short-lived. Watching or participating in sports is a major source of pleasure for many people. So, too, is watching interesting or entertaining programs on television. These sources of pleasure are easily available, and there are many more like them. For example, someone's mood can be lifted considerably if they are asked to describe memories of a happy event in as much detail as possible. But in all these cases the mood can soon pass. The same is true of listening to music, even though this has been found to produce joy, excitement, and even profound satisfaction in some people. The type of music is important—a flowing melody or rhythm combined with a fast pace is the type of music most likely to produce a feeling of joy. Similarly, people are more likely to get up and dance when they hear certain types of music.

Other activities known to lift our mood temporarily include dining out, dressing up in nice clothes, and enjoying success of some kind, whether on the sports field or at work (and "enjoying" is the key word here, rather than letting the stress of it get the better of you). Activities such as telling jokes and giving good news or presents, can work for both giver and receiver.

Although water-skiing can be a spectacular way of enjoying an active life, you don't need to be quite so energetic to have a happy life—a routine brisk walk around the neighborhood could do just as well!

All of these strategies have a fairly short-lived effect, seldom lasting more than an hour, but they can be part of a wider program. The key is to make these strategies a habit, so that we obtain a regular succession of mood boosts. The mood-enhancing effects of any of these kinds of activity are increased still further if we make a deliberate attempt to get ourselves into the appropriate mood, and enter enthusiastically into the spirit of it all. Being fully engaged in what is going on in your own life, and in the world around you, has been shown to be a major factor in happiness and life-satisfaction.

Jogging your way to happiness?

Many research studies have produced evidence that exercise can have a beneficial effect on mood. In 1981, John Griest and colleagues working at the University of Wisconsin reported on a study of patients suffering from a moderate degree of neurotic depression. As treatment, the patients were given either psychotherapy or a graduated program of walking, jogging, and running. When asked about their mood, the psychotherapy group gave self-assessments that were clearly improving gradually as time went on—and so, too, did the exercise group.

One year later, this improvement was still apparent. Also, almost all those in the exercise group had continued with their new interest in jogging. This fits with the observation that a major hurdle where undertaking an enjoyable activity is concerned is getting started; once you're over that, the enjoyment can really build. The patients had needed encouragement to start on the daily program and were helped further by the fact that they were introduced to exercise gently, beginning with walking and then progressing to jogging as they became fitter.

Those on the exercise program were asked to keep a diary of their progress. It seems that, as they improved, they became more and more enthusiastic. Some reported that they looked forward to their daily sessions, partly because they knew they were benefiting from them. Others observed that they felt happier and less depressed for hours after exercise—as if it was generally toning up their system and rejuvenating them.

Other studies have also shown that regular exercise reduces anxiety and depression: as a general rule, fitter people are found to be in better mental health. This is why exercise is becoming a recognized treatment for anxiety and depression, to complement the more usual medication and counseling. (It is also worth noting that the resources involved in exercise make it easily accessible for all kinds of people, and rather more economical than individual psychotherapy.)

Vigorous exercise, such as step aerobics, is excellent, as long as you're fit.

Does drinking make us happy?

Some people are convinced that drinking alcohol is a sure way to improve mood. There may seem to be positive short-term effects, but the full picture is more complex. The harmful side-effects of sustained drinking are well-documented, but people do tend to forget that one of the side-effects of alcohol is a "rebound" situation that is the reverse of happiness and well-being. At the time, a drink seems to lift our mood, but what it is actually doing is slowing down certain nervous-system processes, and this can also make us emotionally depressed slightly further down the line.

Research into the effects of alcohol has produced interesting findings. It seems that the drug has a definite psychological effect— in other words, because we think it will change our mood, it does. The social situations in which people most commonly drink, such as dining out or meeting friends, can certainly help to add to this effect and are probably very important feel-good factors in themselves.

In a typical experiment into the effects of alcohol, volunteers are asked to test the effects of different drinks. They are given either fruit juice with a substantial amount of vodka added, or fruit juice with vodka merely smeared around the glass. Provided they cannot tell the difference, both drinks are likely to make the person more cheerful and sociable and less inhibited. It is the expectation and the situation, rather than the alcohol, that is improving their mood.

Saying is believing

In 1910, a French pharmacist called Emil Coué developed a direct self-help technique based on people saying positive things to themselves as a form of "auto-suggestion." He was responsible for the well-known saying: "Every day and in every way, I am getting better and better."

Despite some success with this approach, Coué's method was not developed further until more than fifty years later. Emmett Velten, a schoolteacher from Memphis, Tennessee, asked his students to read fifty positive statements about themselves, first silently and then aloud. The statements were of the type "Things are looking up" and "My life is getting better." Doing this was found to produce a significant improvement in mood. Although the effect was short-lived (ten to fifteen minutes), it occurred every time the process was repeated. This general approach has become known as the Velten technique, and it is now used widely by psychotherapists.

The Velten technique today

Velten's technique has been refined over the years. For example, the number of statements has been reduced from fifty to twelve, as people are thought to benefit from being allowed more time to concentrate on each statement. Individuals are also encouraged to imagine (or "visualize") themselves in situations that are in keeping with the mood they wish to create—say, sitting by a rippling stream to help reinforce a sense of peace and stillness.

To maximize the chances of a positive effect, sessions are arranged at a suitable time of the day, such as after a day's work, when people are winding down. The Velten approach has echoes and links throughout many therapies—the chanting carried out by some meditation groups, for example.

How hypnotherapy can help

Hypnosis is another therapy—sometimes in the form of "auto-suggestion"—that is widely used to suggest to people that they are feeling happy. In a typical session, patients lie on a couch, are hypnotized by the therapist, and are then told that their mood is improving. Providing they fall fully into a hypnotic state, people do tend to report feeling whatever the therapist suggests to them. Those who are fully trained in self-hypnosis can use this technique on themselves.

Hypnotherapy can be used not just to suggest feelings of greater happiness but also to boost self-confidence and self-esteem, in many cases increasing people's belief in such things as their social skills or ability to deal with difficult work situations.

The therapy often seems to have a general effect in improving a person's overall mood and outlook. For example, subjects may be more charitable than usual in their attitude to others when asked for an opinion; or, when asked to recall memories or tell a story, they will choose more positive ones. When given "free association" tests—where people are asked to say the first thing that comes to mind—hypnotherapy seems to make people find more positive or cheerful links.

So, just how long do these effects last? With most people, the effects of hypnosis in general, whether used to promote happiness or for any other reason, seem to hold only while they are still in a "trance," or at most for a short while (about fifteen minutes) afterwards. Attempts to extend the beneficial effects on a long-term basis to everyday life have been generally unsuccessful, which is partly why hypnosis has not become a standard method of therapy.

Happiness training

One of the relatively new approaches in the field of happiness-seeking is cognitive behavior therapy. This is based on the notion that what is important for our mood is not so much what happens in our life, but how we actually interpret events. A characteristic of unhappy people is that they usually perceive the world in a negative way—their outlook on life is generally gloomy. For example, they tend to exaggerate their failures and blame themselves for just about everything that goes wrong.

Aaron Beck, working in Philadelphia, developed a technique in which patients are trained to change the way they think. They are taught to stop blaming themselves when things go wrong (we all make mistakes), to stop stretching themselves too thinly (we are less likely to fail if we are not too ambitious in the first place), and to become more focused on the present (there is little point in dwelling on the past).

Alongside this attitude-shifting, patients are encouraged to improve the quality of their life. After discussion with the patient, the therapist gives them "homework" tasks, starting with something that will be very easy to achieve. This is where an experienced therapist is indeed important, someone who is a good judge of what the patient is likely to achieve, since it is vital that patients are successful in getting off to a good start. By gradually achieving more and more, patients can see for themselves that things are improving.

The effects of cognitive behavior therapy have been measured in several controlled trials. The results are encouraging, with many patients showing improvement where other methods of treatment have failed. In some trials, cognitive behavior therapy has compared favorably with the best of antidepressant medication. Not only does the attitude of patients improve, but they also begin to lead a more interesting and active life. And, most importantly, the improvement effect seems to be long-lasting. It seems that training people how to develop a positive attitude and to gradually improve their quality of life really can lead to greater happiness.

A characteristic of happy people is that they view the world in a generally positive way. They are not burdened by self-criticism and they don't look for negative aspects of the situation they are in.

Life-events therapy

In Oregon, Peter Lewinsohn pioneered a different branch of happiness-training by developing a therapy based on systematic attempts to structure and improve people's lives. He asked individuals to keep a diary of their reactions to different events during the day. A plan was then formulated to increase those activities that improved their mood.

This commonsense approach really did seem to work. The activities that tended to improve mood were obvious things such as eating good food, doing work well, sitting in the sun, and spending time with happy people. A list was drawn up for each individual, and a check was made to ensure that these activities helped. With suitable planning and counseling to make sure that the patients worked at the therapy, most people enjoyed a daily improvement in mood. However, while moods could improve for the rest of that day, this did not carry over to the next day; it seems we must all ensure that each day contains at least some pleasurable activities.

This anonymous picture shows a coffee house of the seventeenth century. It's often these ordinary things—talking and drinking with like-minded people that can most improve mood.

Lewinsohn's research came up with a comprehensive list of everyday activities likely to help people. Some were effective because they involved pleasant social interactions: being around cheerful people, seeing an old friend or someone you love, feeling popular in a gathering, or being asked for help or advice. Some were effective because of the way they made individuals feel worthwhile: learning to do something new, for example, or being told that you have done well. Other items on the list of activities included looking at beautiful scenery, listening to music, wearing fresh clothes, and eating good meals.

Although mood-enhancing therapies are in the main designed for patients suffering from depression, they do seem to help people in general to enjoy their lives more. In 1977, Michael Fordyce reported a series of studies designed to test the effects of happiness training.

In one of these studies, Fordyce's students were asked to read about the research into happiness and then to apply some of the findings to their own life. In another, they were provided with a list of recommended activities (such as "spend more time socializing") and were asked to select those that appealed to them. They were then asked to incorporate these into their daily lives over a six-week period.

When the results were analyzed, the happiness ratings of the student group were compared with those of another group. This other group had been given a completely different set of tasks to those on the recommended list, but it was suggested to them that these activities "would help them become much happier people."

Overall, the results in favor of Fordyce's "list" approach were sufficiently encouraging for him to establish a list of fourteen recommended activities (or fundamentals as he called them) as a basis for happiness training. The fourteen fundamentals were:

1. Keep busy and be more active
2. Spend more time socializing
3. Be productive at work
4. Get better organized and plan things out
5. Stop worrying
6. Lower your expectations and aspirations
7. Develop positive, optimistic thinking
8. Become present-oriented
9. Work on a healthy personality
10. Develop an outgoing, social personality
11. Be yourself
12. Eliminate negative feelings and problems
13. Remember that close relationships are the number one source of happiness
14. Put happiness as your most important priority

Setting realistic goals

Another approach to improving your satisfaction with life is to focus on setting yourself some realistic goals, and then making sure that they are achieved. People adopting this strategy draw up a list of things that they would like to achieve, and then plan how to go about making them happen. Discovering that these goals are attainable gradually builds confidence and self-esteem.

People also discover that the tasks they set themselves can be intrinsically enjoyable, or at least satisfying when achieved. All this tends to lead to an improved outlook and increased life-satisfaction. Providing that individuals are sensible in choosing goals, a therapist is not essential, although professional guidance is recommended, at least at the beginning. Once off to a good start, this goal-setting approach is a perfect one for people to try on their own.

In a 1990s study involving more than one hundred college students in Japan, Yumiko Nedate and Fujio Tagami compared happiness training using the Fordyce approach with cognitive behavior therapy aimed only at reducing anxiety. Because of the beneficial effects of the Fordyce strategy, they concluded that happiness training was well worth using alongside other psychological therapies.

In 1980, Shelley Lichter, Karen Haye, and Richard Kammann recruited volunteers in New Zealand for four-week happiness training courses. They met twice a week and were trained in one of two ways. In one group, they were trained to recognize the beliefs and attitudes that contribute to happiness—trying to be an optimist, looking on the bright side, and so on. In the other group, they were asked to rehearse positive statements (such as "I feel good about myself") every morning for about ten minutes.

After a month they were tested and compared with a control group of people who were on a waiting list for the course. Compared with this control group, the group who completed the training course rated themselves as happier in various ways. They also had more positive beliefs and felt more satisfied with life in general. Six weeks later, this improvement was still apparent—it had even slightly increased.

This lasting improvement is especially encouraging, since so many treatments have only short-term effects, with many patients relapsing. It seems that the training course had given these New Zealanders new skills that they continued to apply after the course had ended. The control group and those on the course started off at the same level of happiness (indeed they were selected so that this would be the case). After the course ended and six weeks later, the ratings of happiness and satisfaction were much higher for those on the course.

Becoming your own happiness-trainer

Most people do actually know what they should do to become happier, it's just that they never get around to doing it. This is where the new approaches to therapy outlined above come into their own. Rather than just listening to patients and interpreting what they say, some therapists are now actively encouraging their clients to change their lives. It is probably these lifestyle changes, rather than the therapy sessions on their own, that lead to better mental health—and most of us can make changes to our lives for ourselves.

Not many people will get the chance to go on a happiness training course. However, anyone can incorporate much of the advice given in this chapter. Deliberately trying to find ways to increase happiness seems to be the key, along with avoiding things such as setting unrealistically high goals. We should remember that cultivating a positive outlook on life is important, as well as choosing plenty of enjoyable things to do.

We also need to find meaning and purpose in life. For many people, this is most easily achieved through work and leisure, and through maximizing the pleasure we get from our friendships and relationships. For some, meaning and purpose can be found in spiritual and religious fulfillment. All in all, it seems that Aristotle was right to claim that to be happy, we must be virtuous and avoid inner conflict.

14: beyond a warm feeling Sir Anthony Kenny

Two more elements of well-being

...in the pursuit of happiness, no less than in the creation of the world, there lurks a problem of evil. Sir Anthony Kenny

In July 1999, at the Chalet des Anglais in St. Gervais, Switzerland, the Oxford philosopher Sir Anthony Kenny and his economist son, Charles Kenny, conducted a reading party for Rhodes scholars on "Democracy, Development, and Well-Being." In June and July 2000, as his contribution to the *Discovery of Happiness*, Sir Anthony reworked a talk he gave to the Rhodes scholars. He offers it here as the final chapter in our book and as a living illustration that philosophizing about happiness is as much an activity for the twenty-first century A.D. as for the fourth century B.C.

Happiness and well-being

Throughout many ages, philosophers have discussed the nature of happiness. Some placed the concept at the apex of their system of moral philosophy. Aristotle and Bentham, for instance, agreed in so doing, though they had very different conceptions of what constitutes happiness.

Bentham equated happiness with pleasure, conceived as a warm feeling inside; Aristotle made a contrast between bodily pleasure and true happiness, whose highest expression was intellectual contemplation. But for both these philosophers, happiness was a supreme good, which supplied the purpose, and measured the value, of human acting and striving. "From the dawn of philosophy," wrote Bentham's pupil Mill, "the question concerning the *summum bonum*—or, what is the same thing, concerning the foundation of morality, has been accounted the main problem in speculative thought and has occupied the most gifted intellects."

Happiness has also been a cardinal notion in religious thought. Jesus' Sermon on the Mount, one of the founding texts of Christianity, begins with the eight *beatitudes*, which proclaim eight keys to blessedness or happiness. The first three, in the Jerusalem Bible, read as follows:

> *How happy are the poor in spirit;*
> *Theirs is the kingdom of heaven.*
> *Happy the gentle;*
> *They shall have the earth for their heritage.*
> *Happy those who mourn;*
> *They shall be comforted.*   (Mt. 5: 3–5)

Like Christianity, Judaism and Islam regard happiness as a goal of the religious life. "How happy those of blameless life who walk in the law of the Lord," sang the Psalmist (Ps. 119: 1), and the Koran holds out to the true believer the prospect of enduring felicity.

Of course, not all religions are happiness-oriented in this way. Happiness, however differently it may be defined, seems essentially to involve the satisfaction of one's wants; and in Buddhism, release from the sufferings of life is to be sought through the suppression, not the satisfaction, of desire. And the happiness promised to religious people may be placed in the world as we know it (as in much of the Hebrew Bible) or in some future state which is yet to be made manifest (as in Islam and Christianity). The old Catholic catechism, in response to the question "why did God make you?" answered "God made me to know Him, love Him, and serve Him in this world, and to be happy with Him forever in *the next*."

Social psychologists, too, attach importance to happiness and have sought to investigate its nature by asking people how happy they are and trying to correlate the answers with various elements of personality and environment. Psychologists and physiologists have also sought bodily conditions that are associated with agreeable and cheerful mental states. The effects of euphoria-inducing drugs enable correlations of this kind to be established, and thus it has been discovered, for instance, that increased availability of serotonin to the brain is associated with a form of happiness. Few, however, would wish to claim that happiness is nothing other than a particular chemical condition of the brain.

Economics and utility

In recent years, economists—as well as philosophers, preachers, and psychologists—have been taking an interest in the nature of happiness. Of course, ever since Bentham and Mill founded the philosophy of utilitarianism, economists have been keenly interested in the meaning of utility, which for Bentham was identical with pleasure and with happiness. But utility, while an overarching economic concept, has until recently remained a largely unexamined one.

Recently, economists have interested themselves in the independent measurement of happiness. Economic performance, after all, is only a means to an end. "That end," in the words of the economist Andrew Oswald, "is not the consumption of beefburgers, or the accumulation of television sets, nor the vanquishing of some high level of interest rates, but rather the enrichment of mankind's feeling of well-being. Economic things matter only in so far as they make people happier." It is important to find out to what extent economic growth promotes happiness; and in order to find this out, economists have joined with social psychologists in asking people whether or not they feel happy.

The answers to the questionnaires have produced some interesting results. As we have seen in chapter 12, in the United States, while real income raced ahead in the 1970s and into the 1990s, there was no increase in the percentage of those describing themselves as very happy. Similarly, reported levels of satisfaction with life in European countries have varied only very slightly. In 1999, the World Bank economist Charles Kenny concluded a study of this matter with the observation that there is no clear general link between economic growth and well-being—"A certain level of economic well-being is a necessary condition for happiness, but there is plentiful evidence to suggest that economic well-being is far from sufficient. Once a certain standard of living is attained, the relationship between growth and happiness breaks down."

Do questionnaires measure happiness?

In this chapter I am not concerned with analyzing or interpreting the results of recent surveys of this kind. Rather, I want to question the philosophical presupposition of the questionnaires: namely, that self-reporting is an appropriate way of measuring happiness. Economists and psychologists have drawn attention to some of the problems of comparing self-ascriptions in different countries and cultures: there are subtle differences between the meaning of words like happiness, contentment, and satisfaction in English and between their near-synonyms in other languages. But these, it is suggested, are contingent difficulties easily overcome: German-speaking Swiss, for example, can be compared with Germans and Austrians. I want to argue, however, that the difficulty is a more fundamental one that transcends local linguistic differences. Is it really true that individuals are the best authorities on their own happiness? Do I necessarily know whether I am really happy?

The answer to these questions depends on one's underlying conception of happiness. For Bentham and those who think of happiness as a warm feeling the answer is obviously yes. Pleasure and pain are opposites, and it is as natural to take an interviewee's word for it that she

A certain level of economic well-being is a necessary condition for happiness, but there is plentiful evidence to suggest that economic well-being is far from sufficient Charles Kenny, World Bank economist

is very happy as it is to take a patient's word for it that he is in great pain. According to Aristotle, however, like his master Plato, most people are ignorant of the true nature of happiness and therefore do not really know whether they are happy or not. Many people, he said, equate happiness with the enjoyment of sensual pleasure or the possession of political power, or the combination of the two in the life of an oriental despot. In reality, Aristotle believed, the stable and rewarding satisfaction that we all seek is to be found only in the intellectual life of the philosopher. But this key to the nature of happiness is a secret known only to few.

Of course, Aristotle wrote in Greek, not in English, and it might be suggested that his distance from the utilitarian conception of happiness simply shows that "happiness" is not a good translation of his Greek word *eudaimonia*. But this would be altogether too simple. Both Aristotle and Bentham are employing the same fundamental concept of a supreme value that provides the motivation and the measure for human activity. What I want to do is to identify the elements of this concept, which has a role in many different philosophical systems and many different historic cultures, however it may be expressed in the idiom of different languages. To circumvent linguistic difficulties with the word "happiness" I shall speak of "well-being."

Well-being

In the concept of human well-being, I shall argue, there are three distinct elements. I shall call them contentment, welfare, and dignity.

Contentment is what is measured by self-ascriptions of happiness. It is not so much a feeling or sensation as an attitude or state of mind; but of the elements of well-being it is the one which is closest to the utilitarian idea of happiness. If contentment is to amount to a constituent of well-being, it must be an enduring and stable state; not mere temporary euphoria or glow of satisfaction.

Welfare, the most obvious sense of material welfare, consists in the satisfaction of one's animal needs, for food, drink, shelter, and the other things that conduce to bodily flourishing. Self-ascription does not have the same central role in the measurement of welfare as it does in the case of contentment; we may be mistaken about the state of our bodily health and other people are often better placed to make a judgment here.

Dignity is a more complicated notion to define, but we may say initially that it involves the control of one's own destiny and the ability to live a life of one's choice. Because dignity concerns, among other things, one's relationship to other people, there cannot be absolute and objective measurements of dignity as there can of welfare.

These three elements vary independently. Each may exist without the others; and more importantly, pairs of the triad may occur without the third.

It is possible for someone to have welfare and contentment without dignity. A well-housed and well-fed slave who looks for nothing better than his servile lot and has no complaints about the way he is treated, may be thought of as being in a certain sense quite happy.

Contentment and dignity may be present without welfare. A devout and ascetic hermit, revered by all who come in contact with him may regard himself as blessed even though he may be undernourished and unhealthy. If we look for a secular example, we may think of hunger strikers, admired by a throng of supporters, suffering resolutely to further a cause they believe to be paramount. Both religious and secular martyrs have died proclaiming their happiness.

It is easy, too, for welfare and dignity to be present without contentment, as in the case of a bored and pampered member of a rich and dominant elite.

Many of the problems and paradoxes that have perplexed those who have sought to understand the nature of happiness are removed if we resolve it into these separate elements. Let us look closer at each of them in turn.

Contentment

Contentment is a necessary but insufficient condition of well-being. If people are contented with their lot, that does not necessarily mean that their lot is a happy lot. Their contentment may derive from ignorance, or from a false evaluation of alternatives, or from a lack of imagination. We might call such contentment the contentment of the unraised consciousness. In less contemporary idiom we might call it the contentment of the unexamined life, which Socrates thought was not worth living. You may think you are well off and yet not be; equally, you may be well off and not know it. In either case, something is lacking to your well-being.

It is the presence or absence of contentment, rather than of welfare or dignity, which is measured by the responses of those that are the subjects of questionnaires on happiness. Even as a measure of contentment, responses to questionnaires are problematic. Self-ascription may lack sincerity: a person may be too proud to reveal discontent, or too superstitious to boast of happiness. One may belong to a culture, or occupy a status, which is hostile to whingeing or fearful of hubris. Again, self-ascription may lack stability: the euphoric state of mind candidly avowed to the questioner may turn out to be no more than a passing mood. So too may be the depression which leads one to place oneself into the lower of the questioner's response bands.

As has been said earlier, the contentment which is a constituent of well-being must be an enduring, not a momentary, state. But we are not

Les Très Riches Heures du Duc de Berry. **This early fifteenth-century manuscript shows grapes being harvested by apparently contented peasants. Does the possibility that they may have felt more contented than us mean their lives may have been better than ours?**

necessarily good at predicting our own future contentment. King Midas thought that he would be happy if he could turn everything into gold at a touch. As his case shows dramatically, the satisfaction of our wishes does not always lead to contentment. St. Teresa once said that more tears were shed over prayers that had been answered than over prayers that had not been granted.

Despite all the problems, self-ascription does provide a rough and ready measure of contentment. Avowals, however, whether spontaneous or solicited by pollsters, are not the only expressions of contentment. Laughter, smiling, scowling, weeping, posture, comportment, and other forms of behavior give us an indication of others' contentment or discontent; so too the style and energy of their application to their daily tasks. Such behavioral indications provide, to some extent, an objective check on the sincerity of linguistic expressions of subjective contentment. Psychologists, too, claim to have discovered chemical features of the brain which are found empirically to correlate with the verbal and behavioral criteria of contentment. However, contentment is only a single element in well-being.

Of course, contentment is a valuable thing, and for individuals in many circumstances it may be wisest to aim at nothing more: the other elements of well-being may be, through no fault of their own, beyond their reach. If I am going to remain poor and powerless for the rest of my life, I had best count whatever blessings I have. I do well to trim my desires to those that can be satisfied in practice. But if this is a reasonable attitude to take with regard to one's own life, it is surely an inadequate one for those responsible for the well-being of others. As far as possible, we have to ensure not just that others are resigned to their narrow lot, but that they have appropriate options and wide horizons. "They're perfectly happy as they are" is the slogan of the exploiter throughout the ages, whether it is masters exploiting slaves, or males exploiting females, or one racial group exploiting another.

Welfare

I turn from contentment to welfare, the second of the three elements of well-being. Methodologically, welfare is the simplest of the three elements to identify and analyze. It is objective, it is easily measured, and it is universally agreed to be a good and to be a component of well-being. Unambiguous measurements are possible of the caloric intake of individuals, the expectation of life of particular groups, and other parameters constitutive of welfare. Each of us recognizes that medical check-ups may be a more reliable guide to the good or ill condition of our body than any subjective feeling of illness or well-being.

Dignity

In addition to material welfare there is psychological welfare, which is less easy to quantify: freedom from mental illness or defect, and freedom from tragedies occurring within one's family or immediate social circle. Psychological welfare of this kind overlaps, to some extent, the third element of well-being, which we are now to consider. This I have labeled "dignity." It is both more complex and more contentious to analyze. It is related to welfare in the following way: a fundamental element of human dignity is the individual's awareness of his or her absolute and relative position with regard to welfare. Deliberately to keep people in ignorance of this is an affront to their dignity, even if it may increase their contentment. To balance dignity against contentment is a crucial and difficult task for those with responsibility for other people's welfare—nowhere more obviously than when we are considering the situation of the terminally ill.

By "dignity," I should explain, I mean an objective feature of one's situation in life—I do not mean the character trait of fortitude, which might enable one to remain self-possessed in adverse circumstances. So understood, dignity has three elements, which we may refer to in shorthand as choice, value, and prestige. To possess dignity you must have a degree of choice and control over your life, the life that you lead must be a worthwhile one, and it must carry with it a degree of prestige. These three elements are not all on the same level; but all of them must be investigated if we are to assess a person's well-being.

Choices that matter

Even the most downtrodden of us is constantly faced with choices in daily life; but obviously not all choices are significant. The freedom to choose between blue cheese and Thousand Island dressing on one's salad is not a valuable component of liberty or dignity. The three most important choices are the choice of one's cultural identity, the choice of one's social role, and the choice of the political arrangements under which one lives.

It is an important part of dignity that key elements of one's cultural identity—such as one's religion or one's language—are not forced upon one unwillingly from outside. The choice of cultural identity is obviously very largely a matter of consent. We are brought up as part of an ethnic group, with a certain language, customs, morality, and religion; we cannot decide in advance what is to be the culture into which we are born and educated.

What matters is that when we come of age to take responsibility for ourselves, we should willingly identify with that culture, or be able, if we do not, to alter or discard features of it, or to adopt a different one. When it is not our cultural identity, but our social role, that is to be defined, then it is an element of dignity that choice, and not mere consent, should enter in. For this reason there is greater dignity in marriage to a partner of one's choice than in a marriage arranged by one's family and friends. This is so, whether or not an arranged marriage may lead in certain cases to more secure welfare and greater contentment. Again there is greater dignity in working at a job that one has freely contracted to perform than in carrying out duties that are assigned one, willy-nilly, by one's social status.

A third, but in my view less important, constituent of the control of one's life which is an element in dignity is one's degree of participation in the political arrangements under which one lives. A person who has control over the rulers who govern him to the extent that he can help to vote them out in a future election clearly enjoys greater dignity than one who has no such control.

Value

We have identified three elements of the control over one's life which is one of the constituents of dignity. But such control, though necessary, is not a sufficient condition of the kind of dignity that I am talking about. For a life may be totally under one's control, and yet undeserving of respect because dissipated in pointless activities. For the dignity which is of the essence of well-being, a life must involve activities that are worthwhile in themselves and not merely devices to pass the time.

In deciding whether activities are worthwhile, there are subjective and objective factors to take into account. Whether a particular type of work confers dignity depends both on the degree of job satisfaction of the person employed, and on the value placed on it by society. Obviously, many very different types of jobs may provide satisfaction and esteem: but it is an essential element of well-being that the manner in which one provides for the welfare of oneself and one's dependents should not be mere drudgery, work that is tedious and repetitive. Of course, not only work but also leisure is assessed on the scale of dignity, as it ranges from the creativity of an artist to the torpidity of a couch potato. Some philosophers indeed, of an aristocratic bent, have thought that only leisure activities could confer dignity: that paid work was of its very nature degrading. In our own time it is unemployment, rather than employment, that is an affront to one's dignity.

Prestige

In addition to choice and worthwhile activity, the third element which I identified in dignity is prestige. Unlike the other elements of dignity, prestige is not an essential constituent of well-being; but it can undoubtedly contribute to and augment it. Prestige is based on one's possession of goods of a kind that arouse the respect and envy of others. These need not be material goods, but they are bound to be positional goods: goods which relate to one's position in society and which of their nature cannot be universally shared, since—in the words of the light-opera librettist W.S. Gilbert—when everyone is somebody, then nobody's anybody.

Dignity, as I have defined it, is not at all restricted to people occupying positions of wealth and power in economically advanced societies. St. Simeon Stylites—a hermit who spent his life in prayer at the top of a pillar, revered by pilgrims who flocked to assist in his devotions—was a friar who lived a life of his choice, in an activity which he and his society regarded as the most worthwhile of all activities, and who enjoyed the esteem of all his contemporaries. He possessed each of the three elements of the dignity which is a constituent of well-being.

Economic development and well-being

We have now broken down the notion of well-being into three independent items: contentment, welfare, and dignity, and analyzed each of these in turn. Our aim was not to show that no one could be happy who did not score highly on each of these parameters. Throughout history, few have been fortunate enough to be in possession of all the desirable characteristics we have identified. The purpose of the analysis was rather to show that when we pursue happiness for ourselves or others, the goal is not a simple but a complex one, and that if we are trying to measure happiness, a single metric will not suffice. Policies for the maximization of well-being may involve trade-offs between dignity and contentment, between welfare and dignity, and between contentment and welfare.

Happiness, as we said earlier, is a topic that has recently attracted the attention of economists—and development economists in particular. Their interest is focused on the question: to what extent does economic development promote well-being? The way to answer the question is clearer, now that we have separated out the different ingredients of well-being. If we think of development as being the technological facilitation of the achievement of desirable goods, it is clear that this will be related in different ways to the different elements we have distinguished.

In short, whoever you may be
To this conclusion you'll agree
When every one is somebodee
Then no one's anybody! Gilbert and Sullivan

Questionnaire-based empirical studies enable us, with all the caveats entered earlier, to relate development to contentment. The correlations that have been found suggest that development assists contentment to the extent that it assists welfare. Once a certain level of per capita income has been reached in a country, further growth appears not to lead to further contentment. However, even in rich countries development can help dignity by removing drudgery. The provision of washing machines and dishwashers has given possibilities for fuller lives to those doing housework, even in the richest of countries. While resignation may be a virtue, it can be exercised in nobler contexts than in that of washing dishes. But of course, affluent householders in the developed nations have much less to complain of than the breadwinners of the third world, and the fact that domestic appliances can make a genuine contribution to their well-being does not mean that their provision should have priority over the satisfaction of the basic welfare needs of the poor.

Democracy and well-being

Philosophers and politicians sometimes address the question: does democracy promote happiness? Here again, in order to answer the question, we have to distinguish between the different elements of well-being. I have suggested earlier that a degree of control over the way in which one is governed is a factor which contributes to one's dignity; and therefore, to the extent to which dignity is a crucial element in well-being, some form of democracy is not just a cause but a constituent of well-being. But the more interesting inquiry is whether democracy is a positive causal factor in the production of welfare and contentment.

To answer this question we must once again make distinctions, but this time in relation not to the concept of happiness but to the concept of democracy. There are several separable features which make up the democratic institutions that are prized in first-world countries. Most important are the basic human rights of freedom from torture and degrading treatment by government: without these rights, welfare, dignity, and contentment are all under threat. But there are other important features of political arrangements which are less immediately connected with the elements of well-being. One is the citizens' ability to choose and change governments by elections. Another is the independence of incorrupt courts. Another is a market that functions effectively.

Many economists claim that a market operating in comparative freedom is the most effective agent for the production of national wealth. If this is so, then since there is undoubtedly a strong link between wealth and health which is the core of welfare, the freedom of the market can claim to be an important causal factor in the generation of that element of well-being. And an effective market depends on effective government to

Sir William Nicholson
(1872–1949),
The polling station.
Giving citizens the right
to vote is one way of
conferring dignity.

maintain civil order, and impartial courts to enforce commercial contracts. Hence the preference for capitalist democracy among economists concerned to promote well-being.

Maximizing well-being

While the free-market economy may be the most efficient tool so far discovered to provide the means of welfare, it does not necessarily follow that it maximizes contentment. There are several reasons for this. In the first place, once basic needs have been satisfied, many people are more concerned with dignity than welfare, and the operation of the market may diminish—rather than increase—the dignity of those engaged in it. Members of traditionally dignified professions may feel insulted if their services are rated simply at market value. The great inequalities which the free operation of the market allows to build up may cause great discontent among those at the lower end of the scale, even if in absolute terms their income is large enough to provide them with adequate welfare. Some economists have gone so far as to claim that it is relative, not absolute, income which is the determinant of happiness. Though this is an exaggeration, in 1999, Charles Kenny reported evidence that roughly equal income distribution is a positive factor in happiness understood in terms of contentment.

Some philosophers regard inequality of wealth as being in and of itself an affront to human dignity. For my part, I do not see why I should regard myself as at all degraded simply because some other people are very much richer than I am. If the existence of billionaires is the price to be paid for an economic system that is the most efficient method of generating wealth for all of us, then it is a price I am willing to pay—but then, since all my basic needs are well satisfied, perhaps I am not the kind of person whose judgment matters. In any event, if the free operation of the market is the most efficient method of reducing absolute poverty, we should not oppose it simply because it may mean that a man with only two yachts will be unhappy because his neighbor possesses three. What matters in judging the merits of societies and economic systems is not so much the spread of incomes, as the absolute level of those who are least well treated by the system. Of course, those with great wealth may use their economic power to bring other people into a condition where their welfare and dignity is genuinely compromised. They may also be seriously at fault by not using their wealth to improve the lot of the poorest. But heartlessness and exploitation are not necessary concomitants of riches.

Once one has analyzed well-being into its elements, as I have tried to do here, one sees that with the best will in the world, there cannot be a policy which will maximize everything that is involved in our intuitive notion of happiness. Some years ago, I wrote an essay on individual happiness in which I made a distinction between satisfaction and fulfilment. I wrote:

> *In assessing happiness we have regard not only to the satisfaction of desires but also to the nature of the desires themselves. The notions of contentment and of richness of life are in part independent, and this leads to paradox in the concept of happiness, which involves both. Plato and Mill sought to combine the two notions, by claiming that those who had experience of both inferior and superior pleasures would be contented only with the superior pleasures of a rich intellectual life. This, if true, might show the felicity of Socrates satisfied, but will not prove that Socrates dissatisfied is happier than a fool satisfied. The greater a person's education and sensitivity, the greater his capacity for the "higher" pleasures and therefore for a richer life; yet increase in education and sensitivity brings with it increase in the number of desires, and a corresponding lesser likelihood of their satisfaction. Instruction and emancipation in one way favor happiness and in another militate against it. To increase a person's chances of happiness, in the sense of fullness of life, is… to decrease his chances of happiness, in the sense of satisfaction of desire. Thus in the pursuit of happiness, no less than in the creation of a world, there lurks a problem of evil.*
>
> Sir Anthony Kenny, *The Anatomy of the Soul*

Using a threefold rather than a dual analysis of the elements of happiness, and concentrating on the happiness of groups rather than of individuals, does nothing to contradict the conclusion that there can be no simple recipe for the maximization of happiness. But this does not mean that we cannot seek ever better systems of trade-offs to protect and promote the well-being of the inhabitants of the planet.

Glossary

Aristotelianism
A comprehensive philosophical system based on the writings of the Greek philosopher Aristotle (384–322 B.C.), which became available in Europe in the thirteenth century and dominated university teaching of philosophy and science until well into the seventeenth century.

Babylon
An ancient city and kingdom in Mesopotamia.

Cartesianism
A philosophical system based on the writings of the French philosopher and scientist René Descartes (1596–1650), who inaugurated our modern conception of philosophy. He did this through his conviction that knowledge must not be founded on the authority of the ancients, but rather constructed from the bottom up, by going back to first principles. He held that the passions could be controlled through a scientific understanding of their physiological basis.

cognitive behaviour therapy
Any therapy for improving mood and satisfaction with life by training the patient to interpret events and to appraise self-worth and the worth of others in a more positive light.

Confucianism
Philosophy and system of government based on the ideas of Confucius (c.551–479 B.C.), a Chinese political philosopher. In addition to dominating Chinese government and philosophy until the end of the empire in 1911, Confucianism influenced all of the East Asian and many Southeast Asian nations, including Japan after the seventh century A.D.

Cynics
A Greek philosophical sect that flourished from the fourth century B.C. into Christian times and was distinguished more for its unconventional way of life than for any system of thought. Cynics opposed social

conventions (including family life) and attempted to return to a natural life by renouncing property and citizenship.

Daoism
(from the chinese word *dao* meaning "road" or "way") Chinese philosophy advocating humility, harmony, and religious piety.

Eleatics
Greek philosophers of the fifth century B.C. from the southern Italian city of Elea (including Parmenides and Zeno of Elea) who asserted that reality is necessarily described as one unique, uncreated, indestructible, and immovable whole.

Enlightenment
A European intellectual movement of the seventeenth and eighteenth centuries in which ideas concerning God, reason, nature, and man were synthesized into a world view that instigated revolutionary developments in art, philosophy, and politics. Central to Enlightenment thought were the use and the celebration of reason. The goals of rational man were considered to be knowledge, freedom, and happiness.

Epicureanism
A philosophical system based on the writings of the Athenian philosopher Epicurus (c.341–270 B.C.), who believed in the exclusively material nature of reality and regarded pleasure as the highest good. It died out in the late Roman empire, but was modified and brought into line with Christianity in the mid-seventeenth century.

eudaimonia
Greek for "happiness", "the good."

Fall
The succumbing of Adam and Eve to temptation and its consequences as described in Genesis.

Form
In the writings of the Athenian philosopher Plato (427– 347 B.C.) the ideal of any given type of thing. The Form is grasped by the intellect alone through intuition, and the particular instances of that type of thing met in experience are reflections of it, lacking its perfect reality.

Fu
Chinese term for happiness, good fortune.

Gothic

A style of art, decoration, and architecture prevalent in western Europe in the twelfth to sixteenth centuries, characterized by stained glass and highly linear and stylized arches, sculpture, and painting.

Habad-Lubavitch Hasidic group

A Hasidic group originating in Russia and later moving headquarters to New York, noted for its zeal in fostering Jewish religious life through supporting schools, orphanages, and study groups. The Habad branch of **Hasidism** is known by an acronym of the Hebrew names of the first three **sefirot**, which mean "Wisdom," "Understanding," and "Knowledge."

Halachah

Jewish law, largely about living a Jewish life.

Hasid, pl. Hasidim

A follower of **Hasidism**.

Hasidism

The Jewish spiritual movement founded by Rabbi Israel Baal Shem Tov in eighteenth-century eastern Europe.

hedonism

The pursuit of pleasure as the highest good, from the Greek word *hedone* meaning "pleasure."

humanism

A scholarly movement which began in the fourteenth century and was concerned with the recovery, interpretation, and imitation of ancient Greek and Roman texts, along with the archeological study of the physical remains of classical antiquity. As the Renaissance progressed, it turned into a dynamic cultural program influencing almost every facet of intellectual life until the seventeenth century.

Huo

Chinese term for ill fortune.

Kabbalah

Literally, "received [tradition]." Jewish mystical teachings, particularly of the variety which began to be taught in medieval Spain.

Kabbalist

An exponent of the Kabbalah.

Le
Chinese term for happiness, joy.

Life events therapy
Therapy that attempts to restructure the life of patients to include more positive day to day events, such as eating good food, doing work well, sitting in the sun, and being with happy people.

lokayata
Ancient Indian philosophy of "those who follow the world." It combined **naturalism** and **hedonism**.

manas
Sanscrit term—approximated by "heart" or "mind"—for a place where feelings of happiness and suffering are experienced.

materialist
Any philosophy that asserts the reality of the material world.

Middle Ages
A period of almost a thousand years in European history from the fall of the Roman empire in the west, through fifth-century barbarian invaders, to the **Renaissance**.

moksa
See *nirvana*

monotheism
The belief in the existence of a sole god, as opposed to polytheism, the belief in the existence of a number of gods, and atheism, the denial of the belief in any god.

Naturalism
In philosophy, any view that implies that human experience and material reality can be fully understood without any recourse to supernatural explanations.

Neo-Confucianism
A rationalistic revival of Confucian philosophy in the eleventh century A.D. that exercised profound influence on Chinese thought for the next eight hundred years with its emphasis on loyalty, social structure, and social order.

Neoplatonism

A late development of Greek philosophy that mixed elements of the older systems, especially Plato's, with mystical speculation about the relation of God to humans and the universe.

nirvana

In Buddhism, perfect bliss and release attained from the extinction of individuality.

oligarchy

Government by a small group of people.

Orphism

Greek religious cult focused on Orpheus, a mythical model of the human become divine through ascetic self-denial and the cultivation of the mind.

Peak experiences

Deeply satisfying states of mind identified by the American psychologist Abraham Maslow as characteristic of people who have achieved **self-actualization.**

Platonism

A philosophical system based on the writings of the Athenian philosopher Plato (427-347 B.C.), who regarded the material world as a shadowy imitation of an unchanging immaterial reality (the **Forms**), to which the soul would return when freed from its imprisonment in the body.

Ptolemaic system

A theoretical model of the universe describing the positions and apparent motions of the sun, moon, and planets, formulated by the Alexandrian astronomer and mathematician Ptolemy about A.D. 140.

Pythagoreans

Ancient Greeks who aimed to live in accordance with the teachings of the sixth-century mystic Pythagoras. According to these, the intellectual life, rather than the life of the body, would bring the soul into harmony with the natural order. One means to this end was the practice of ritual purification through the contemplation of numbers. The term was also applied to fifth-century mathematicians and astronomers influenced by Pythagorean ideas.

Renaissance

The period from the fourteenth to sixteenth centuries that saw a rebirth of Greek and Roman learning in Europe.

Sanskrit

Ancient language of India in which Hindu scriptures are written.

Sefirah, pl. Sefirot

In Kabbalism, spiritual manifestation of the Divine

Self-actualization

In the theories of the American psychologist Abraham Maslow, the self-fulfilment that becomes possible for people who—having solved the problems of basic material welfare, security, love and friendship, and self-esteem—can focus attention on creative self-expression and other non-urgent needs, such as the appreciation of beauty and knowledge.

serotonin

A body chemical that occurs especially in the brain, where it acts as a neurotransmitter (a compound that released by one brain cell stimulates others with receptors for the compound).

Shiva

One of the principal Hindu deities. He is both destroyer and restorer, the great ascetic and the symbol of sensuality, the benevolent herdsman of souls and the wrathful avenger.

stigmata

Marks corresponding to those left on Christ's body by the Crucifixion, said to have been impressed by divine favor on the bodies of St. Francis of Assisi and others.

stoa poikile

(Greek: "painted porch") An open space in a building of ancient Athens called the Agora. It served as a meeting ground for religious, political, judicial, social, and commercial activity.

Stoicism

A philosophical system founded by the Greek philosopher Zeno of Citium (334–262 B.C.) and later developed by Roman thinkers such as Seneca (A.D. c.1–65). Virtue was the only good and the passions were to be repressed. Happiness was to be achieved through acceptance of God's will. Known throughout the **Middle Ages** and the **Renaissance**, it experienced a revival in the late sixteenth century and stayed in fashion for roughly another hundred years.

sukha

Sanskrit term for happiness.

Talmud
The rabbinical compendium of Jewish law, lore, and commentary.

theism
The belief in the existence of gods or a god that can be supernaturally revealed to man and who sustains a personal relation to his creatures.

tikkun
"Repair." In Kabbalistic teachings, the task of bringing repair and unity to the spiritual dimensions of existence. This will result in the coming of the Messiah.

Unitarian
A person who believes that God is not a Trinity but one person and advocating that religion should be free from formal doctrine.

Upanisads
A series of philosophical compositions concluding the exposition of the Vedas—orally preserved hymns, formulas, and incantations of India (c.1500–500 B.C.).

Utilitarianism
A philosophical viewpoint that holds that the principle of an action's moral rightness or wrongness is whether it helps to maximize happiness.

Velten technique
Therapy, named for the American psychologist Emmett Velten, that consists of patients saying positive things to themselves—such as, "Things are looking up," and "My life is getting better"—as a form of auto-suggestion.

Vishnu
One of the principal Hindu deities, worshiped as the protector and preserver of the world and restorer of moral order.

Zohar
("Book of Splendor") The most important work of Jewish mysticism, whose influence for a number of centuries rivaled that of the Old Testament and the **Talmud**.

Further reading

Chapter one

Argyle, M., *The Psychology of Happiness*, London, 2001
Ekman, P., and Friesen, W.V., *Unmasking the Face*, Englewood Cliffs, 1975
Kenny, Anthony, *The Anatomy of the Soul*, Oxford, 1973
Kenny, Anthony, *Aristotle on the Perfect Life*, Oxford, 1992

Chapter two

Auboyer, Jeannine, *Daily Life in Ancient India, from 200 B.C. to A.D. 700*
(translated by Simon Taylor), New York, 1965
Basham, A. L., *The Wonder that was India* Part 1, London, 1956
Biardeau, Madeleine, *Hinduism: The Anthropology of a Civilization*, Delhi,
1989
Chattopadhaya, Debiprasad. *Lokoyata: A Study in Ancient Indian
Materialism*, Bombay, 1978
Collins, Steven, *Nirvana and Other Buddhist Felicities: Utopias of the Pali
Imagination*, Cambridge, 1998
Hiriyanna, M., *Outlines of Indian Philosophy*, London, 1932
Thapar, Romila, *A History of India*, Harmondsworth, 1956

Chapter three

Allinson, Robert E., *Chuang-Tzu for Spiritual Transformation*, Albany, 1989
Bauer, Wolfgang. *China and the Search for Happiness* (translated by
Michael Shaw), New York, 1976
Chan, Wing-tsit, *A Source Book in Chinese Philosophy*, Princeton, 1963
Confucius. *The Analects* (translated by D. C. Lau), Harmondsworth, 1979
Fung Yu-lan, *A Short History of Chinese Philosophy*, New York, 1997
Lao Tzu, *Tao te Ching* (translated by D. C. Lau), Harmondsworth, 1963
Wang Keping, *The Classic of the Dao: A New Investigation*, Beijing, 1998

Chapter four

Annas, Julia, *An Introduction to Plato's Republic*, Oxford, 1981
Barnes, J., *Early Greek Philosophy*, London 1987
Guthrie, G. H., *Greek Philosophy*, Cambridge, 1962–81
Kenny, Anthony, *The Aristotelian Ethics*, Oxford, 1978

Long, A. A., *Hellenistic Philosophy*, Berkeley, 1986
Nussbaum, Martha C., *The Fragility of Goodness,* Cambridge, 1986
Plato, *The Republic* (translated by Desmond Lee) Harmondsworth, 1987

Chapter five

Altmann, A., *Studies in Religious Philosophy and Mysticism*, London, 1969
Davidson, H., *Alfarabi, Avicenna and Averroes on Intellect: Their Cosmologies, Theories of the Active Intellect, and Theories of Human Intellect*, New York, 1992
Goodman, L. E., *Jewish and Islamic Philosophy. Crosspollinations in the Classic Age*, Edinburgh, 1999
Hyman, A. and J. J. Walsh (eds), *Philosophy in the Middle Ages. The Christian, Islamic, and Jewish Traditions*, Indianapolis, 1973
Kraemer, J. (ed.), *Perspectives on Maimonides*, Oxford and London, 1991
Maimonides, *The Guide of the Perplexed* (translated by S. Pines in 2 vols.), Chicago, 1963
Nasr, S. H., and O. Leaman (eds.), *History of Islamic Philosophy*, London, 1993

Chapter six

Hallamish, Moshe, *An Introduction to the Kabbalah* (translated by Ruth Bar-Ilan and Ora Wiskind-Elper), Albany, 1999
Jacobson, Simon, *Toward a Meaningful Life, The Wisdom of the Rebbe Menachem Mendel Schneerson*, New York, 1995
Lamm, Norman, *The Religious Thought of Hasidism, Text and Commentary*, New York, 1999
Majeski, Shloma, *The Chassidic Approach to Joy*, New York, 1995

Chapter seven

Abdel-Kader, A.H., *The Life, Personality and Writing of al-Junayd*, London, 1976
Arberry, A.J., *Sufism: An Account of the Mystics of Islam*, London, 1950
Attar, Farid ad-Din, *The Conference of the Birds* (translated by D. Davis and A. Darbandi), London, 1984
Attar, Farid ad-Din, *Muslim Saints and Mystics* (translated and edited by A.J. Arberry), London, 1979
Nicholson, R.A., *Studies in Islamic Mysticism*, Richmond, Surrey, 1994
al-Qushayri, *Principles of Sufism* (translated and edited by B.R. von Schlegell), Berkeley, 1990
Rumi, Jalal al-Din, *Mystical Poems* (translated by A.J. Arberry), Chicago and London 1968
Schimmel, A., *Mystical Dimensions of Islam*, Chapel Hill, North Carolina, 1975

Smith, M., Rabi'a: *The Life and Work of Rabi'a and Other Women Mystics in Islam*, Oxford, 1994

Sviri, S., *The Taste of Hidden Things: Images on the Sufi Path*, Inverness, California, 1997

Chapter eight

Evans, Joan (ed.), *The Flowering of the Middle Ages*, London, 1985

de Hamel, C., *A History of Illuminated Manuscripts*, Phaidon, 1994

Ladurie, E. LeRoy, *Montaillou: Cathars and Catholics in a French Village, 1294-1324*, Harmondsworth, 1978

Leyser, H., *A Social History of Women in England, 450-1500*, London, 1996

Reynolds, S., *Fiefs and Vassals*, Oxford, 1994

Southern, R. W., *The Making of the Middle Ages*, London, 1993

Chapter nine

Kraye, Jill, (ed.), *The Cambridge Companion to Renaissance Humanism*, Cambridge, 1996

Røstvig, Maren-Sofie, *The Happy Man: Studies in the Metamorphoses of a Classical Ideal, I: 1600-1700*, second edition, New York, 1962

Schmitt, Charles B. et al., (eds), *The Cambridge History of Renaissance Philosophy*, Cambridge, 1988

Trinkaus, Charles, *Adversities Noblemen: The Italian Humanists on Happiness*, New York, 1965

Chapter ten

Gay, Peter, *The Enlightenment: An Interpretation*, London, 1973

Mill, J.S. and Bentham, Jeremy, *Utilitarianism and Other Essays* (edited by Alan Ryan), Harmondsworth, 1987

Plamenatz, John, *The English Utilitarians*, Oxford, 1966

Shaw, William H., *Contemporary Ethics: Taking Account of Utilitarianism*, Oxford, 1999

Sidgwick, Henry, *The Methods of Ethics*, 1874, reprinted Indianapolis, 1981

Smart, J.J.C., and Williams, Bernard, *Utilitarianism For and Against*, Cambridge, 1973

Chapter eleven

Argyle, M., *The Psychology of Happiness*, London, 2001

Bradburn, N.M., *The Structure of Psychological Well-Being*, Chicago, 1969

Eysenck, M.W., *Happiness: Facts and Myths*, Hove, 1994

Headey, B., and Wearing, A., *Understanding Happiness*, Melbourne, 1992.

Kahneman, D., et al (eds.), *Well-Being: The Foundations of Hedonistic*

Psychology, New York, 1999
Wessman, A.E., and Ricks, D.F., *Mood and Personality*, New York, 1966

Chapter twelve
Argyle, M., *The Social Psychology of Leisure*, London, 1996
Argyle, M., T*he Psychology of Happiness*, London, 2001
Bradburn, N.M., *The Structure of Psychological Well-Being,* Chicago, 1969
Cochrane, R., *Handbook of Life Stress, Cognition and Health*, Chichester, 1988
Eysenck, M.W., *Happiness: Facts and Myths*, Hove, 1994
Kahneman, D., et al (eds.), *Well-Being: The Foundations of Hedonistic Psychology*, New York, 1999
Thayer, R.R., *The Biopsychology of Mood and Arousal*, New York, 1989
Veenhoven, R., *Correlates of Happiness*, Rotterdam, 1994

Chapter thirteen
Argyle, M., *The Social Psychology of Leisure*, London, 1996
Argyle, M., *The Psychology of Happiness*, London, 2001
Eysenck, M.W., *Happiness: Facts and Myths*, Hove, 1994
Kahneman, D., et al (eds.), *Well-Being: The Foundations of Hedonistic Psychology*, New York, 1999
Thayer, R.R., *The Biopsychology of Mood and Arousal*, New York, 1989

Chapter fourteen
Kenny, Anthony, *The Anatomy of the Soul*, Oxford, 1973
Kenny, Anthony, *Aristotle on the Perfect Life*, Oxford, 1992

index

Picture acknowledgements

Every effort has been made to trace all present copyright holders of the material used in this book, whether companies or individuals. Any omission is unintentional and we will be pleased to correct any errors in future editions of this book.

p.10 Sandro Vannini/CORBIS, p.19 Horace Bristol/CORBIS, p.28 Philadelphia Museum of Art/CORBIS, p.53 Earl & Nazima Kowall/CORBIS, p.64 Library of Congress/ CORBIS, p.83 Bettmann/CORBIS, p.100 Dave Bartruff/CORBIS, p.106 Angelo Hornak/CORBIS, p.108-109 K.M.Westermann/CORBIS, p.116 Gianni Dagli Orti/CORBIS, p.122 Archivo Iconografico, S.A./CORBIS, p.132 Sandro Vannini/CORBIS, p.160 Leonard de Selva/CORBIS, p.165 Burstein Collection/CORBIS, p.181 Bettmann/CORBIS, p.184 Richard Bickel/CORBIS, p.194 Bettman/CORBIS, p.202 Dave G.Houser/CORBIS, p.208 Ted Spiegel/CORBIS, p.211 Rick Doyle/CORBIS, p.212 Duomo/CORBIS, p.217 Bettmann/CORBIS;

p.13 British Library, London, UK/Bridgeman Art Library, p.15 Derby Museum & Art Gallery, Derbyshire, UK/Bridgeman Art Library, p.17 The Fine Art Society, London, UK/Bridgeman Art Library, p.24 Christie's Images, London, UK/Bridgeman Art Library, p.27 Victoria & Albert Museum, London, UK/Bridgeman Art Library, p.30 Private Collection/Bridgeman Art Library, p.33 Victoria & Albert Museum, London, UK/Bridgeman Art Library, p.34 Victoria & Albert Museum, London, UK/Bridgeman Art Library, p.43 Bibliotheque Nationale, Paris, France/Bridgeman Art Library, p.51 Bibliotheque Nationale, Paris, France/Bridgeman Art Library, p.56 Musee Conde, Chantilly, France/Giraudon/Bridgeman Art Library, p.59 Louvre, Paris, France/Peter Willi/Bridgeman Art Library, p.61 Christie's Images, London, UK/Bridgeman Art Library, p.69 Biblioteca Nazionale, Turin, Italy/Bridgeman Art Library, p.70 Louvre, Paris, France/Giraudon/Bridgeman Art Library, p.72 Museo Archeologico Nazionale, Naples, Italy/Bridgeman Art Library, p87. Bibliotheque Nationale, Paris, France/Topham Picturepoint/Bridgeman Art Library, p.92 Private Collection/Bridgeman Art Library, p.111 British Library, London, UK/Bridgeman Art Library, p.115 Chester Beatty Library, Dublin/Bridgeman Art Library, p.119 British Library, London, UK/Bridgeman Art Library, p.120 Private Collection/Bridgeman Art Library, p.144 S.Ambrogio, Florence, Italy/Bridgeman Art Library, p.147 Galleria degli Uffizi, Florence, Italy/Bridgeman Art Library, p.131 British Library, London, UK/Bridgeman Art Library, p.129 San Francesco, Upper Church, Assisi, Italy/Bridgeman Art Library, p.136 Private Collection/Bridgeman Art Library, p.138 Biblioteca Nazionale, Turin, Italy/Bridgeman Art Library, p.142-143 Vatican Museums & Galleries, Vatican City, Italy/Bridgeman Art Library, p.150 Noortman, Maastricht, Netherlands/Bridgeman Art Library, p.155 University College Museum, London, UK/Bridgeman Art Library, p.158 Capitol Collection, Washington, USA/Bridgeman Art Library, p.169 Private Collection/Bridgeman Art Library, p.193 Phillips Collection, Washington DC, USA/Bridgeman Art Library, p.197 Musee de l'Orangerie, Paris, France/Peter Willi/Bridgeman Art Library, p.205 National Gallery, London, UK/Bridgeman Art Library, p.218 British Museum, London, UK/Bridgeman Art Library, p.222 Josef Mensing Gallery, Hamm-Rhynern, Germany/Bridgeman Art Library, p.229 Victoria & Albert Museum, London, UK/Bridgeman Art Library, p.235 The Stapleton Collection/ Reproduced by permission of Elizabeth Banks/Bridgeman Art Library;

Penny Brown: p.36, p.38, p.39 p.85, p.175 ;

p.44-45 The Art Archive/Freer Gallery of Art, Washington, p.148 The Art Archive/Musee Cernuschi, Paris;

Mary Evans Picture Library: p.66 , p.78, p.88, p.125, p.135, p.152, p.162-163, p.172; Mary Evans Picture Library/Explorer Archives: p.80

p.67 Stuart McCready, p.99 EK Tiefenbrun, p.102 Private Collection, p.103 Private Collection, p.104 Zalman Kleiman (d.1985), courtesy of the Hasidic Art Institute, Brooklyn, p.84-85 By permission of The British Library, YT36 folio169, p.95 By permission of the British Library, add.man.14761.folio.2.verso

Copyright © MQ Publications Limited, 2001

Design concept: Broadbase
Design: Bet Ayer
Picture Research: Suzie Green

Sourcebooks, Inc.
P.O. Box 4410, Naperville, Illinois 60567–4410

Tel: (630) 961–3900
Fax: (630) 961–2168

Library of Congress Cataloging-in-Publication Data

The discovery of happiness / edited by Stuart McCready.
    p. cm.
  Includes bibliographical references and index.
  ISBN 1-57071-674-9 (alk. paper)
    1. Happiness. I. McCready, Stuart.

  BJ1481 .D57 2001
  170--dc21   00-066165

Printed and bound in Italy

1 2 3 4 5 6 7 8 9 0

ISBN: 1-57071-674-9